D0726160

The Open University

Block 4
Slavery and freedom

Bernard Waites and Amanda Goodrich

This publication forms part of the Open University module A200 *Exploring History: Medieval to Modern 1400–1900*. Details of this and other Open University modules can be obtained from the Student Registration and Enquiry Service, The Open University, PO Box 197, Milton Keynes MK7 6BJ, United Kingdom (tel. +44 (0)845 300 60 90; email general-enquiries@open.ac.uk).

Alternatively, you may visit the Open University website at www.open.ac.uk where you can learn more about the wide range of modules and packs offered at all levels by The Open University.

To purchase a selection of Open University materials visit www.ouw.co.uk, or contact Open University Worldwide, Walton Hall, Milton Keynes MK7 6AA, United Kingdom for a brochure (tel. +44 (0)1908 858793; fax +44 (0)1908 858787; email ouw-customer-services@open.ac.uk).

The Open University
Walton Hall
Milton Keynes
MK7 6AA

First published 2007

Second edition 2011

Copyright © 2007, 2011 The Open University

All rights reserved. No part of this publication may be reproduced, stored in a retrieval system, transmitted or utilised in any form or by any means, electronic, mechanical, photocopying, recording or otherwise, without written permission from the publisher or a licence from the Copyright Licensing Agency Ltd. Details of such licences (for reprographic reproduction) may be obtained from the Copyright Licensing Agency Ltd, Saffron House, 6–10 Kirby Street, London EC1N 8TS (website www.cla.co.uk).

Open University materials may also be made available in electronic formats for use by students of the University. All rights, including copyright and related rights and database rights, in electronic materials and their contents are owned by or licensed to The Open University, or otherwise used by The Open University as permitted by applicable law.

In using electronic materials and their contents you agree that your use will be solely for the purposes of following an Open University course of study or otherwise as licensed by The Open University or its assigns.

Except as permitted above you undertake not to copy, store in any medium (including electronic storage or use in a website), distribute, transmit or retransmit, broadcast, modify or show in public such electronic materials in whole or in part without the prior written consent of The Open University or in accordance with the Copyright, Designs and Patents Act 1988.

Edited and designed by The Open University.

Printed and bound in the United Kingdom by Bell & Bain Ltd, Glasgow

ISBN 978 1 8487 3911 6

2.1

MIX
Paper from
responsible sources
FSC
www.fsc.org   FSC® C007785

CONTENTS

WHAT YOU NEED TO STUDY THIS BLOCK

- Units 13–16
- *Module Companion*
- *Media Guide*
- Anthology: Gibbons, R.C. (ed.) (2007) *Exploring History 1400–1900: An Anthology of Primary Sources*, Manchester, Manchester University Press/Milton Keynes, The Open University
- A200 website
- DVD 2
- TMA 04

Learning outcomes

When you have finished this block, you should be able to:

- understand the origins, persistence and overthrow of New World slavery
- understand the reasons for the racial character of New World slavery
- understand the economic significance of slavery and the slave trade to Britain.

Further, more specific, learning outcomes are given at the beginning of each unit of this block.

Amanda Goodrich and Bernard Waites

INTRODUCTION

'Slavery' and 'freedom' are among the most emotive words in our vocabulary. This block should help you understand why they resonate so powerfully in our culture. So far in A200 you have studied western European history. Now, we turn to the Atlantic 'world' created by European colonisation, transatlantic trade and the forced migration in European vessels of millions of African slaves to plantation colonies in the Caribbean and American mainland. This form of slavery is termed 'chattel slavery', and defines the ownership of one human by another. New World[1] or Atlantic slavery was the most extensive, productive and profitable system of chattel slavery in history; it was also unique in being exclusively black. Such slavery is, then, significant not only from a humanitarian viewpoint but also from an economic one.

Block 4 will range over two centuries and touch on four continents, so the first thing you should do is familiarise yourself with the map of the Atlantic 'world' (Figure 13.1) and the chronology on the A200 website. In this block you will be studying slavery primarily in terms of economic history. This involves the study of quantitative data (numbers and statistics) as well as qualitative evidence. You may not feel very confident about handling such data but don't worry, this block helps you through the material. You may be surprised to discover that economic history also engages with moral, political and social issues and connects closely with other genres of history. Moreover, economic history opens up interesting ways of viewing change over time – here the transition from medieval to modern – and it is fundamental to understanding this transition, in which slavery and the slave trade played an important part.

This unit introduces the historical context of slavery and the slave trade. It aims to show that slavery took place at a period of considerable economic, social and political change, culminating in events such as the French Revolution and in processes such as the Enlightenment and the Industrial Revolution, which generated new ideas about the nature of modern life. This unit will help you to understand how slavery fits into history from medieval to modern.

Your study here moves on from what is termed the early modern period to the eighteenth and nineteenth centuries. Historians identify this period with a shift towards 'modernity'.

---

[1] In this block, 'New World' and 'the Americas' are used interchangeably, the Caribbean sea is taken to be part of the Atlantic ocean and the Caribbean islands belong to 'the Americas'.

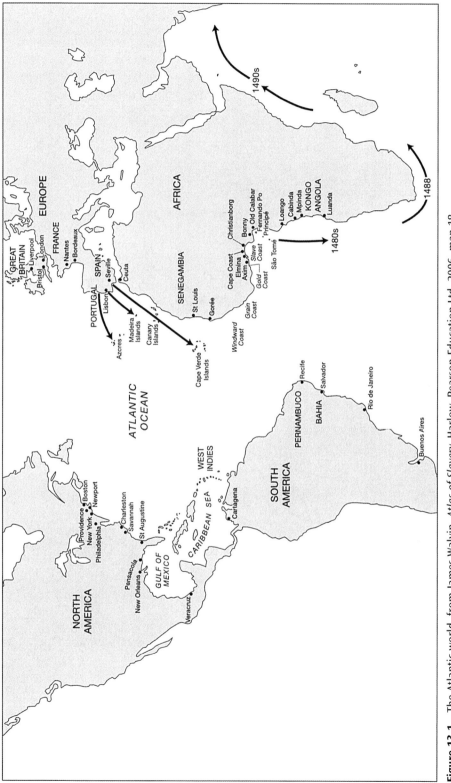

Figure 13.1 The Atlantic world, from James Walvin, *Atlas of Slavery*, Harlow, Pearson Education Ltd, 2006, map 18

EXERCISE

Briefly write a list of the elements of change that you might identify with 'modernity'. If you need to, re-read the discussion of modernity in the *Module Companion* before drawing up your list.

Spend about 20 minutes on this exercise.

DISCUSSION

This is a difficult exercise and for that reason we are proceeding directly to a discussion, rather than giving a specimen answer. Your list may include a variety of ideas: modernity is hard to define and there are many interpretations of it. What we might consider 'modern' today does not necessarily reflect what historians mean by the term and there is much debate among historians about how to define our period and other periods. What follows is a list of elements that may be identified with 'modernity' in the eighteenth and nineteenth centuries. It is not, of course, exhaustive, but it does include major aspects of change.

Economic change:

- growth of industrialisation
- expansion of European capitalism
- development of political economy (this could also be included under the heading of 'intellectual change')
- development of commerce
- expansion of overseas markets
- demographic change and urbanisation
- emergence of a consumer society.

Political change:

- radical reform politics emanating from the French Revolution and a change in the role of ordinary people in politics
- move towards greater political engagement, particularly by the emerging middle class
- development of the nation state
- move towards democracy.

Intellectual change:

- development of Enlightenment ideas focused on reason and rationality
- growth in the importance of science triggered by the Enlightenment
- increasing adherence to ideas about individual rights and liberty.

Social change:

- growth in the press and printing
- increased secularisation and decline of the confessional state
- changes in the way people worked and lived, particularly in relation to urbanisation and industrialisation
- increased individualism.

As the above list illustrates, our period is associated with much change and not all of it peaceful. Indeed, this was a period of considerable upheaval and turmoil, political and social, and some historians have termed it 'the age of revolutions' (e.g. Hobsbawm, 1993 [1962]). Certainly a number of 'revolutions' have been identified between the late seventeenth and early nineteenth centuries, including the early agricultural and financial revolutions, political American and French revolutions, scientific, industrial and consumer revolutions. How far each such development amounted to a revolution is a matter of some debate but it is clear that considerable changes took place.

As you will see, the above changes that are listed as associated with modernity developed alongside and informed each other. Nevertheless, it is also important to note that they did not always pull in the same direction. Atlantic slavery reflects the complexities of the concept of 'modernity'. To adopt slavery might seem to be a regressive step for European societies moving towards greater modernity: we often associate slavery with backward societies. But, as a system of economic production, New World slavery exhibited several characteristics that we associate with modernity. Technical efficiency was one: sugar and cotton plantations have, for example, been aptly dubbed 'factories in the field' because of the way they coordinated and exploited human labour. Atlantic slavery also reflected modern systems of commerce, utilising systems of credit, insurance, shipping and world markets.

Moreover, an important aspect of modernity is individual freedom. Today we tend to view freedom as the right to live our lives without interference as long as we do not break the law; the right to act, speak and think freely.

| EXERCISE | Now find the Credo Reference website (under Reference in the online collections on the Library website). You may recall that you visited Credo Reference in Block 1. There is guidance on finding Credo Reference on the module website if you need it. |

Type 'freedom' into the search box and you should be presented with a choice of sources. Scroll down the list until you find the entry from *A Glossary of Political Theory* and consider what it says about freedom.

Spend about 20 minutes on this exercise.

| DISCUSSION | As this definition suggests, today the concept of freedom is complex and has become highly controversial. Until the development of liberalism in the nineteenth century, the concept of freedom was not generally considered to be applicable to all. The Enlightenment articulated the concept of freedom as a universal right and the American and French revolutions enshrined this natural right common to all humanity in their early constitutions. Yet despite such moves towards modernity, slavery and freedom were interdependent in the English-speaking Atlantic world, where people dedicated to political and personal freedom established repressive slave systems that made slavery hereditary. Manumission was not common in the British colonies and the American states. At the outbreak of the American Revolution in 1775, slavery was a legal institution in all thirteen American colonies and their Declaration of Independence was written by a slaveholder. Indeed, in the eighteenth century it was not unusual to find the same person advocating both freedom and slavery with unruffled conscience. |

One example is John Locke (1632–1704), a political philosopher and an important intellectual influence on both the 'Glorious' and the American revolutions. As you learned in Block 3, in the seventeenth century those opposed to the absolutist pretensions of the Stuarts could be found arguing that freedom is the natural condition of humankind. From this state of nature all human beings derive certain inalienable rights; that is, rights that cannot be relinquished in any circumstances. Slavery violates such rights in a number of ways. The ownership of slaves by a master violates the inalienable right to self-preservation, allowing masters to appropriate the slaves' labour, and violates their right of self-ownership, for we are all entitled to what Locke called property in one's own person. The opening page of Locke's *Two Treatises of Government* states:

> Slavery is so vile and miserable an Estate of man ... that 'tis hardly to be conceived, that an Englishman, much less a Gentleman, should plead for't.
>
> (Locke, 1967 [1690], p. 1)

Yet Locke developed his theory of freedom while deeply implicated in the institutionalisation of slavery in the American colonies. In the 1670s, he drafted or helped draft 'The Fundamental Constitutions of the Carolinas', in which it is stated:

> Every freeman of Carolina shall have absolute power and authority over his negro slaves, of what opinion or religion whatsoever [i.e. irrespective of whether the slaves were baptised Christians].
>
> (Davis, 1970, pp. 137–8)

The American Constitution signed on 17 September 1787 provided the basic political parameters for the formation of the United States of America. Whether or not slavery was permitted was left to the individual states and, as you probably know, a rough divide developed between the increasingly 'free states' of the North and those in the South, where slavery persisted until the 1860s. This block will help you understand the paradox of slavery persisting in Anglo-American societies where increasingly the basic principle of state formation was political liberty. Concepts such as 'modernity' and 'freedom', although linked, do not always develop in unison or in a clear linear trajectory through history. Atlantic slavery provides a significant example of how modernity and individual freedom did not coexist in the eighteenth century. This is an issue you should keep in the back of your mind as you study this block.

HISTORICAL CONTEXT

Slavery is the focus of this block, but it is important to study it within the context of its time. Block 3 concluded at the end of the seventeenth century and so here you need to gain some understanding of the eighteenth century and the world within which slavery functioned. This unit focuses primarily on the economic context, although we will briefly consider other historical contexts too. The political context is discussed more fully in Block 5, Unit 17.

As you have seen above, industrialisation was an important factor in the shift to modernity. Essentially this reflects a move from a primarily agricultural society towards an industrial one. But there is much debate among historians as to the pace and extent of industrialisation throughout Europe, and within Britain, and such changes did not occur at the same time in all geographical areas. Indeed, to varying degrees during the eighteenth century and into the nineteenth, much manufacture was still carried out in many areas by hand in small workshops or even in the home; cottage industries were still common. Britain was the first European country to embark on the industrialisation process in the eighteenth and nineteenth centuries. France and Germany followed, and Russia industrialised at the end of the nineteenth century. Those countries that industrialised later tended to do so more quickly.

Since the early twentieth century, historians have debated whether and when Britain experienced what has been labelled an 'Industrial Revolution' and how such a term might be defined. A number of historians and economists identified an Industrial Revolution in terms of a factory-based, mechanised, industrialisation and economic 'take-off' commencing in the second half of the eighteenth century.[2] They suggested that this revolution brought major technological innovation along with change in the structure and conditions of the workforce. Later historians questioned this idea of a sudden economic 'take-off', identifying a longer, slower process. As David Cannadine put it: 'The British industrial revolution is now depicted ... as a limited, restricted, piecemeal phenomenon' and that 'less happened, less dramatically than was once thought' (Cannadine, 1987, pp. 162, 183). Others claimed that there was a 'discontinuity' in the transformation from a primarily agricultural to a primarily industrial society. You will be considering the Industrial Revolution in Britain and the historiographical debate more fully in Unit 15.

Moreover, historians studying industrialisation have adopted different methodologies and debate has developed as to the merits of quantitative or qualitative methods. Economic historians have made an important contribution to understanding by analysing quantitative data from the time. But while such quantitative evidence is valuable, some historians have questioned its reliability. The economic historian Julian Hoppit, in an article entitled 'Counting the Industrial Revolution' in the *Economic History Review* (1990), considered the value of producing an entirely quantitative interpretation of the Industrial Revolution. Hoppit argued that while taking such an approach makes an important contribution to understanding, it also has limitations. For this period quantitative data is scarce, and what is available is often unclear and inexact. This renders calculation difficult and resulting tables and estimates are likely to have a significant margin of error. Nevertheless, Hoppit concludes

---

[2] This model of industrialisation has been associated particularly with W.W. Rostow (1960) in his *The Stages of Economic Growth*.

that quantitative data plays an essential part in interpreting the Industrial Revolution, but that it is imperative also to make full use of available qualitative sources and interpretations (Hoppit, 1990, p. 189). The article highlights the wide variety of sources used by economic historians, such as data on industrial production and output, excise records, social and occupational structure, demographic trends and burial records.

Despite the debates among historians over the nature and pace of industrialisation and the methodologies adopted, there is now some consensus on the issue. It is widely accepted that, in the eighteenth and early nineteenth centuries, a growing industrialisation incorporated loosely connected developments in technical innovation and regional specialisation in manufacture, the growth of markets, structural change in the workforce, entrepreneurial activity and capital formation. Closely linked to such developments are investment in infrastructure, the increase in consumption and the expansion in trade, both at home and abroad, which led in part to the imperialism you will be studying in Block 6. These changes were facilitated by increased agricultural productivity, demographic change and population growth, and also by the financial systems, banking, the availability of credit, insurance and the development of the stock market, which emerged in Britain in the Financial Revolution of the 1690s. The slave trade was one commercial activity that benefited from such financial systems. Historians also generally agree that both quantitative and qualitative methodologies are necessary to an understanding of industrialisation. Maxine Berg and Pat Hudson have written a useful article on this topic, 'Rehabilitating the Industrial Revolution', that should help your understanding of historical debates about industrialisation and provides a valuable interpretation of these debates. In addition, the following exercise will give you useful practice in downloading an electronic journal article from an online reference.

EXERCISE

Now download Maxine Berg and Pat Hudson (1992) 'Rehabilitating the Industrial Revolution', *Economic History Review*, vol. 45, no. 1, pp. 24–50 from JSTOR. You can find guidance on doing this on the module website.

Read the first section of the article, pp. 24–7 up to 'transformation in these years'. Try to summarise the authors' argument.

Spend about 30 minutes on this exercise.

DISCUSSION

Berg and Hudson emphasise the significance of the transformation associated with industrialisation and the importance of social and political aspects, as well as economic, in this process. They show that while historians have challenged the concept of an 'Industrial Revolution' by charting the slow nature of change, some contemporaries thought they were living through a period of rapid transformation. Berg and Hudson consider that significant changes did occur and that the Industrial Revolution should be rehabilitated.

Urbanisation was also an important factor in the move towards modernity. In our period, urbanisation grew rapidly, with some people leaving the land to seek work for wages in towns and cities, thus providing a ready workforce for manufacturers. This does not mean, however, that agriculture ceased to be important in economic terms or that the majority left the land to work in urban environments. Agricultural systems and practices also experienced technological development and the modernisation of methods and practices that helped to feed the growing population. But the opportunities for the labouring poor to live off the land in the traditional way declined, and this contributed to a markedly increased urbanisation. In England, major changes in agricultural practice began towards the end of the seventeenth and early eighteenth centuries. In the rest of Europe such changes took place somewhat later: in the mid to late eighteenth century in France, Germany and Switzerland and during the nineteenth century in Austria, Italy and Russia.

England was the most rapidly urbanising society of its day, accounting for nearly three-quarters of urban European population growth between 1750 and 1800. The transatlantic slave trade contributed to the growth of ports such as Liverpool and Bristol, and Manchester's wealth was largely based on the slave trade and on slave-grown cotton. As a result of industrialisation, traditional kinship ties began to loosen, particularly in the growing towns and cities. Work for wages became the norm and the division of labour (where workers perform a specific task or tasks in the production process) became increasingly common with industrial development. In the later years of our period, we can see the development of what is termed the 'working class' – an urban, labouring workforce, employed in manufacture and services for wages. In Block 5 you will learn more about the effects of rapid urbanisation on the lives of the working class.

With industrialisation and urbanisation came an increase in consumption. Indeed, historians have identified something of a 'consumer revolution' in the eighteenth century, with growth in both the supply of and demand for goods. The pace and timing of this 'revolution' is also debated by historians but it is clear that by the mid eighteenth century many people in England took for granted consumer goods such as pottery, books and foodstuffs, and were coming to live in what we would now call a consumer society. Proportionately fewer did so in Scotland and Wales because living standards were lower. Britain, though more particularly England, was the wealthiest country in Europe. The landed aristocracy was unquestionably the nation's ruling class, but in the cities and towns merchants, shopkeepers, lawyers, apothecaries, master craftsmen, brewers, confectioners and a host of other tradesmen constituted a large and growing socially open 'middling sort'. The middle ranks of society, with family incomes between £50 and £200 a year, comprised nearly 25 per cent of the population by the 1780s (Brewer, 1997, p. xxvi). There were, of course, staggering disparities of wealth, but between the extremes of riches and poverty had emerged a large class of moderately prosperous property holders able to enjoy what Adam Smith (1993 [1776]) and others called the 'decencies' of life, including exotic foodstuffs, snuff and imported goods from the colonies, such as sugar and tobacco from the West Indies, produced by slaves. The emerging middle class were the social backbone of a polite and commercial people for whom shopping and shopkeeping had become vital socio-economic activities. Tax officials recorded 141,700 retail outlets in England and Wales in 1759, of which 21,603 were in London. Urban space was reconfigured to accommodate shoppers. Fashionable shops clustered in brightly lit, well-paved shopping streets, such as the Strand, where shopkeepers developed the art of window display (Brewer, 1997, p. xxvii). But as more labourers began to work for wages in towns and cities they too became greater consumers, mostly of what were termed the 'necessities' of life, and increased demand for such products. Items that they might previously have grown or made for themselves, such as foodstuffs, bread or clothing, they now tended to buy from the many small general stores that could be found in urban neighbourhoods.

These changes in the way people lived and worked have been associated with secularisation and individualism (these terms are discussed in the *Module Companion*). Through much of the module so far you have studied the theme of beliefs and ideologies primarily in terms of religious belief, but here the emphasis shifts towards other forms of ideology: cultural, political and economic. One of the sources of ideology utilised by abolitionists was the pan-European Enlightenment, which flourished between *c*.1680 and *c*.1780.

EXERCISE	Go to Oxford Reference Online, find *The Oxford Dictionary of Literary Terms* and search for 'the Enlightenment'. (You can find further guidance on the module website.) Read the first item that comes up from this dictionary and consider how we might associate the Enlightenment with modernity.
	Spend about 15 minutes on this exercise.
SPECIMEN ANSWER	As the item shows, the Enlightenment is closely associated with modernity and its viewpoint was optimistic, reformist and humanitarian. Enlightenment thinkers believed that people have the potential to improve themselves and their environment and to make the world a better place.
	This item gives a good summary of the Enlightenment and you might wish to print it out for later reference during this module.

Adam Smith (1723–1790), a key figure in the Scottish Enlightenment, came to enjoy considerable influence throughout Europe, particularly for his *An Inquiry into the Nature and Causes of the Wealth of Nations* (1776), which was published in many editions and emphasised the importance of political economy. For governments the manifestation of political economy was the emergence of economic policy. Smith argued that such economic policy should benefit both the people and the state. He also argued that in a commercial exchange each individual acted out of self-interest; a butcher or baker did not provide their products out of benevolence. But this self-interest was ameliorated by the 'hidden hand' of the market, which, so long as free competition was allowed, would ensure that the result would be for the general good. Smith linked Enlightenment ideas with economics and played an important role in introducing a concept of political economy that we associate with modernity. He claimed that 'commerce and manufactures gradually introduced order and good government, and with them, the liberty and security of individuals, among the inhabitants of the country'. Indeed, 'what all the violence of the feudal institutions could never have effected, the silent and insensible operation of foreign commerce and manufactures gradually brought about' (Smith, 1993 [1776], pp. 107, 110). And Smith famously promoted a free market. As we shall see in Unit 16, some of his economic ideas were also influential in bringing about slave emancipation. Contemporaries were proud of the economic developments of their time and, in common with Smith, linked them to Enlightenment ideas about progress and a contemporary sense of modernity. They saw economic changes as important in realising Enlightenment ideals about the freedom and improvability of humankind. Indeed industrialisation, increased wealth and consumption and the concomitant development of ideas were viewed very much as part of a great forward march of progress in which politics and economics were closely linked (a view which you will remember from the *Module Companion* we now identify as a Whig interpretation).

Our period saw a move away from the early modern European state discussed in Blocks 1 and 3 and towards what we might term more modern forms of government. Block 5 will explore the issue of state formation in more detail. The eighteenth century was a period of unrest and disorder, political and social. The period was marked by two revolutions, one in America (*c.*1776–1885) and the other in France (*c.*1789–99), which resulted, eventually, in the demise of absolutism in France and the establishment of new republican governments in both countries. These revolutions triggered discussion around the western world, including Britain, about the nature and role of government and the Christian church. Political thinkers such as Thomas Paine (1737–1809) published works promoting concepts of universal natural rights and the rights of the people to choose their own government, to have a role in politics. If you recall, you came across agitation for parliamentary reform by radical political groups such as the Levellers in Unit 11. It is important, however, not to create false connections with hindsight between one such movement and those that come later. Although the system of government changed hardly at all in Britain before 1832, there was growing popular political awareness and agitation for reform. We tend to think that in the past, power was held by the few and that government functioned entirely in a 'top down' direction. It is true that in the eighteenth century few had the right to vote or were qualified to sit in the House of Commons, and that Britain was ruled primarily by an aristocratic elite. That does not mean, however, that ordinary people had no say in politics. As you will see in Unit 16, there are a number of ways in which ordinary people could gain a political voice, and they were often assisted by a burgeoning press and print industry. Certainly, there were increasing calls both for reform of government and for greater religious toleration for nonconformists, who were excluded from holding public office and, usually, the electoral roles. It is important to understand the movements for the abolition of slavery within the context of this fervent political unrest. It helps, in part, to explain the rather halting progress of abolition we will be considering in Unit 15. Religious toleration came with the repeal of the Test and Corporation Acts in 1828 and the passing of the Catholic Emancipation Act 1829 that together enabled Protestants and Catholics to take public office and, if they otherwise qualified, to vote in elections. Limited political reform was granted under the Reform Act 1832. The franchise was extended from about 440,000 voters to about 656,000, something like 18.4 per cent of English males but far fewer in Scotland and Ireland (O'Gorman, 2003 [1997], p. 369). With political reform in 1832 came slave emancipation a couple of years later. These changes suggested that British ideas about freedom of the individual, which we associate with modernity, were on the rise. However, as you will see, they were not universally applied.

BLOCK 4 AND THE MODULE THEMES

In terms of the three module themes, the main focus of Blocks 1–3 was beliefs and ideologies and state formation. In this block, and particularly in Units 14 and 15, the theme of producers and consumers is dominant. The principal impetus behind Atlantic slavery was economic: its purpose was profit. The slave trade was of great economic significance to Britain and to other European countries, the Americas and indeed to Africa. Over the centuries, slaves performed many social roles: they were concubines, domestic servants, soldiers and administrators, as well as productive workers. But New World slaves were, in the great majority, commodity producers, cultivating export crops (principally sugar but also tobacco and raw cotton) on plantations established solely for that purpose. Most household slaves also lived on plantations as domestic servants to the plantation managers and owners. A slave embodied an investment made by a particular type of capitalist: the plantation owner. Slaves were not cheap and the life expectancy of a slave newly arrived in the Americas was relatively short; the slave owner had to calculate whether the expected returns from the slave's labour in their lifetime would cover both the purchase price and the maintenance costs. Whether to use some of that labour producing the slaves' subsistence was another important calculation owners had to make. In the Caribbean, the profit from sugar was sometimes so great that it paid slave owners to import food for their slaves. Commodity markets were the nexus (or link) between slave producers and European consumers.

Unit 14 first looks at the overall dimensions of the Atlantic slave trade and you will use quantitative data as sources of study. You were introduced to historical statistics in the Block 3 exercises on the Compton Census on the module website; you might like to glance back to guidance provided there to remind yourself how historians use statistics. Quantitative data is of importance in assessing what actually happened in the past. In this unit you will be using tables to calculate the number of slaves shipped across the Atlantic, which nation's traders shipped them and where they were shipped to. This will give you a good picture of how the Atlantic slave trade developed during our period. Moreover, the more we learn from statistics about how many slaves were shipped across the Atlantic, how many per ship, how many lived and died and the price they fetched on arrival, the better we can grasp the inhumanity of the trade.

Unit 14 also covers the interesting issue of the role that Africans played in enabling the slave trade. You might be surprised to discover that Africans were not entirely victims in the slave trade in Africa but also engaged with it and indeed controlled it. As the unit makes plain, this African agency has to be understood in the context of its time and place.

Unit 15 considers the contribution slavery made to economic development in Britain and here you will assess the value to the British economy of the commodities produced in the New World. This unit also engages with two 'revolutions' in our period; the industrial and the consumer revolutions. It considers how far the slave system contributed to industrialisation in Britain: was it a major force that thrust industrialisation forward or was it one of many contributors to economic growth? This is a subject of some debate and you will be comparing the views of a number of historians. The role of New World slavery in the consumer society in Britain is also explored here. West Indian sugar became a popular and widely available commodity for the first time in the eighteenth century. You will study data to assess per capita sugar consumption in our period and primary sources which suggest that, even though sugar was relatively expensive, increasingly the labouring poor became accustomed to regularly drinking sweetened tea. The economic modernity of New World slavery should become clear as you study Unit 15.

Despite the emphasis in Units 14 and 15 on economics as the driving force behind Atlantic slavery, there was also an ideological impetus. Unit 14 explores the ideological rationale for enslaving black Africans – namely, Christian beliefs and evidence gleaned from the Bible. Similarly, slavery was not abolished for purely economic reasons but also, as Unit 16 illustrates, for ideological ones. Christianity was again significant here and evangelical[3] Christians were instrumental in bringing slavery to an end. The American abolitionists, who sought to abolish the institution of slavery throughout the Union, were also in the main evangelical Christians. Christianity was not, however, the only ideology to be invoked by those wishing to bring slavery to an end. As Unit 16 shows, Enlightenment thinkers' identification of a universal

---

[3] The Anglo-American evangelicalism of the later eighteenth and nineteenth centuries had doctrinal affiliations with the evangelical reform movement you studied in Block 2 – especially the doctrine of salvation by faith alone – but also differed from it in key respects. Perhaps the most important was that, whereas evangelical reform began as a movement within the universal Catholic Church, later evangelicalism represented a moral current within Anglicanism and other Protestant sects.

human nature and concern with common human rights influenced attitudes to African slaves and the move towards abolition.

State formation is not a significant theme in this block, but Unit 14 discusses the commercial organisation of the slave trade. Before sovereign states were formed in the Americas, colonial slavery had an oblique relationship with the formation of European states and colonial empires through the commercial policies and practices termed 'mercantilism'. In Unit 16 you will study the slave rebellion in St Domingue that resulted in the formation of a new state, the Haitian Republic, in 1804. Moreover, as you have seen, the movements in Britain to abolish the slave trade and slavery did not occur in isolation, but against a backdrop of changing ideas and calls for political reform in America, France and Britain.

The block's written materials are complemented by two television programmes on DVD 2: 'Sugar dynasty' and 'Breaking the chains'. Here you will be studying a different sort of source but you still need to use critical analysis when interpreting the programmes (see the *Module Companion* for a brief discussion of the presentation of history on television and in film). These programmes are presented primarily as drama and were made for terrestrial prime-time broadcasting. They are, however, based on legitimate historical sources and are historically accurate. Academic historians advised on the scripts, but the finished programmes exhibit some of the drawbacks of a medium that has to entertain as well as inform. In short interviews on your DVD, Professor Gad Heuman, a leading authority on slavery studies, discusses the programmes with Bernard Waites; what he says should sharpen your critical appreciation of them. Of course the programmes are selective in terms of what is included and what is left out. All history, written or visual, must necessarily be selective but perhaps film more so. Thus it is important that you view the programmes within the context of the other sources and materials you come across in this block. 'Sugar dynasty' provides an engaging and informative prelude to the block as a whole and you will be asked to watch this at the beginning of Unit 14 although it also links closely to Unit 15. 'Breaking the chains' dramatises the Jamaican slave rebellion of late December 1831, which proved to be a prelude to the abolition of British colonial slavery in 1834. In Unit 16, you will examine testimony taken from slaves who participated in that rebellion, so the relationship between your written module materials and the television image could scarcely be tighter. *Breaking the Chains* is best viewed in close conjunction with Unit 16.

REFERENCES

Berg, M. and Hudson, P. (1992) 'Rehabilitating the Industrial Revolution', *Economic History Review*, vol. 45, no. 1, pp. 24–50.

Brewer, J. (1997) *The Pleasures of the Imagination: English Culture in the Eighteenth Century*, London, Harper Collins.

Cannadine, D. (1987) 'British history: past, present, and future?' *Past and Present*, vol. 116, pp. 131–72.

Davis, D.B. (1970) *The Problem of Slavery in Western Culture*, London, Pelican.

Hobsbawm, E.J. (1993 [1962]) *The Age of Revolution, 1789–1848*, London, Abacus.

Hoppit, J. (1990) 'Counting the Industrial Revolution', *Economic History Review*, New Series, vol. 43, no. 2, pp. 173–93.

Locke, J. (1967 [1690]) *Two Treatises of Government*, vol. 1 (ed. P. Laslett), 2nd edn, Cambridge, Cambridge University Press.

O'Gorman, F. (2003 [1997]) *The Long Eighteenth Century: British Political and Social History, 1688–1832*, London, Arnold.

Rostow, W.W. (1960) *The Stages of Economic Growth: A Non-Communist Manifesto*, Cambridge, Cambridge University Press.

Smith, A. (1993 [1776]) *An Inquiry into the Nature and Causes of the Wealth of Nations* (ed. L. Dickey), Indianapolis, Hackett.

Bernard Waites and Amanda Goodrich

Learning outcomes

When you have finished this unit, you should be able to:

- understand the dimensions of the Atlantic slave trade

- understand how the intercontinental market for slaves functioned and how slave prices moved over time

- understand the beliefs and ideologies that legitimated the enslavement of black Africans

- understand the demography of the slave trade

- interpret quantitative data

- debate the slave trade's impact on African societies.

INTRODUCTION

DVD exercise

By way of an introduction to this block, you should now watch 'Sugar dynasty' on DVD 2. Before you do so, think about the important issue of evidence and its reliability in relation to the genres of television and film (briefly discussed in the *Module Companion* and Unit 13). 'Sugar dynasty' claims that it is based on contemporary written accounts, such as Beckford of Somerley's, and that it is historically accurate. But remember, films such as this are dramatisations, intended to entertain as much as inform. They cannot provide all the evidence needed to understand the history and economics of the slave trade. You should bear these points in mind as you watch the programme, which should give you a feel for some of the issues related to slavery that you will be studying. As you watch, take brief notes on the following issues:

- the slave experience and the treatment of slaves on Jamaican sugar plantations

- the attitudes to slaves expressed by whites in the film

- the expenditure and investment of plantation profits in both Jamaica and Britain, particularly by the Beckfords.

The programme lasts about 1 hour. You will need your notes to complete the following exercises, and you should also keep them for future reference.

EXERCISE

What were the main features of the slave experience in Jamaica?

Spend about 20 minutes on this exercise.

SPECIMEN ANSWER

Here are some examples:

- On arrival in Jamaica, slaves were sold at 'scrambles' where planters would fight for the best slaves. Prices varied considerably from £5 to £100, depending on age, gender, physique, health and sugar prices. Those who were not purchased because of poor health or physique were called 'refuse' slaves and were often abandoned in the streets to die.

- Slaves were given a new name on arrival on a plantation. Those on the Beckford plantations were all given the surname Beckford. Such a renaming may well have had a profound effect on the slaves' sense of self, their identity, much of which they had already left thousands of miles away.

- Life on the plantations was hard, and infant mortality was high. Many women miscarried or gave birth to a stillborn child, and many children died in their first three years.

- Work in the cane fields was long, hard and backbreaking, and in the sugar boiling house work, though skilled, was hot, arduous and dangerous.

- Punishments were harsh and included whippings, mutilations and even execution for those who tried to escape.

- Slaves were encouraged to be self-sufficient in food and often went hungry.

- Female slaves were the victims of sexually predatory planters.

DISCUSSION

There are many points you could have included, and your list may be different from the specimen answer. In fact, this was in part an exercise on selecting material. It is important when writing analytical essays of the type required in history that you pay careful attention to the relevance of the material you select for inclusion. You might also have noted that we gain a particularly vivid picture of the harsh existence of slavery from film. For example, much can be relayed in one short scene depicting slave punishment.

EXERCISE

Now go back to your notes and see what evidence of planter and other 'white' attitudes to slaves you can find.

Spend about 15 minutes on this exercise.

SPECIMEN ANSWER

There is not as much material concerning white attitudes, but here are some examples:

- Beckford of Somerley stated that the climate and high levels of disease rendered European workers unsuitable for work in Jamaica; Negro slaves were better suited. There was, however, a need to continuously replenish the supply of slaves due to loss through disease and death. He thought that those bred on the West Indian Islands made the best slaves as they were born into slavery and so accepted it.

- The contemporary historian Edward Long explained that planters believed Negro women did not need midwives to assist them in childbirth any more than an orang-utan or any other wild animal.

- Somerley suggested that slave punishments were accepted among the planter community. But he lamented that the slaves had no sense of anticipation and so punishment was always a shock to them.

- To planters the sugar production was more important than the welfare of the slaves. This was illustrated, in particular, by evidence that those who caught their hands in the sugar processing machinery lost a hand rather than the machinery being halted to allow the hand to be removed as this would slow down the sugar processing.

- Planters justified slavery by suggesting that it was not such a bad existence. Somerley protested that slaves in the fields did not work overly hard, except at harvest time, and had Sunday off. Some argued they were no worse off, better off even, than the poor in Britain.

- Planters saw slaves as their property to be used as they wished; the rape of slave women is evidence here. The planter Thomas Thistlewood left details of his sexual activities with slaves in diaries of his life in Jamaica.

- In Britain there was some condemnation of the brutality of the planters and their lack of morality in the treatment of women slaves. Those who visited plantations from Britain were sometimes concerned about the hard life, hours worked and lack of moral and Christian guidance given to slaves.

DISCUSSION

Such material enables us to gather some preliminary evidence about attitudes to slaves among white planters. As far as planters were concerned, slaves were their property to treat as they chose. It was necessary to treat slaves harshly in order to get the work done and make a profit. Treatment was justifiable because slaves were considered to be more similar to animals than to white humans, both physically and mentally. Clearly, writers such as Edward Long reinforced such planter attitudes. We also learned on the DVD that the treatment of the slaves was to some extent influenced by population; there were approximately 20,000 whites and 200,000 slaves on the island of Jamaica in the late eighteenth century. Fear on the part of whites drove the harsh control they inflicted on the slaves.

EXERCISE

Finally, watch the interview between Bernard Waites and Gad Heuman on DVD 2 and consider what is said about the evidence used in this film. Bearing in mind Gad Heuman's critical comments on the programme's confused chronology, how would you explain one Beckford cousin dying a bankrupt while the other was celebrated as the richest man in England? Turn back to your notes on 'Sugar dynasty' and consider how the Beckford of Fonthill's wealth was invested.

Spend about 15 minutes on this exercise.

DISCUSSION

This exercise doesn't have a straightforward answer. The impression is a contradictory one. Sugar profits afforded Beckford of Fonthill a fabulous lifestyle, yet did not keep his cousin Beckford of Somerley out of the debtors' gaol. In his thirteen years on Jamaica, Somerley made money but ultimately ended up in debt and had to leave. We have no reason to think that Somerley was an incompetent businessman and, since he directly managed his property, he was less prey to fraud than absentee planters. What the programme does not make clear is that he arrived in Jamaica when plantation profits were touching an all-time low, chiefly because the American War of Independence impeded the Atlantic slave trade but also because a series of devastating hurricanes had hit the island. The estimated annual profit rate on an admittedly small sample of Jamaican plantations was only 3 per cent in 1776–82, far below the rate of return on domestic trade and manufacturing. Thus it was outside factors that affected his profit rather than bad management. The DVD also suggests that credit arrangements were severely disadvantageous to planters, so they could lose their plantation for a comparatively small debt, which is what happened to Somerley.

Beckford of Fonthill was from a wealthier branch of the family that was on Jamaica much longer than Somerley's thirteen years, and his father had diversified into domestic commerce, finance and politics. This branch weathered the lean years of the 1780s and then garnered huge profits after sugar prices rose with the St Domingue revolution and the outbreak of war between Britain and France. As you will see in Unit 16, St Domingue had been a major producer of sugar until 1791, when rebellion took hold and led to the formation of the Republic of Haiti in 1804. This took St Domingue out of the sugar market, prices rose and planters on other sugar producing islands profited. Annual profits on Jamaican slave plantations were an estimated 13.9 per cent in 1792–98 and 9.6 per cent in 1799 and 1819 (Ward, 1978). No domestic industry or trade earned this rate of profit over more than 25 years. Fonthill invested his wealth in culture, architectural extravaganzas, conspicuous consumption and, briefly, politics. We do not know how typical this pattern of investment was, and Heuman did suggest that some plantation profits were invested in business in Britain. But the judgement made many years ago that West Indian wealth financed more Fonthills than factories has not yet been seriously challenged.

As you work through the rest of the block, consider how evidence is provided in different forms and from different sources, and compare some of the evidence you come across with that provided in 'Sugar dynasty'.

THEMES OF STUDY

This unit relates closely to the themes of producers and consumers, and beliefs and ideologies.

Before the 1830s, the transatlantic trade in African slaves represented the largest overseas migration in history. For sheer persistence, no other branch of European maritime commerce has rivalled it: the first cargo of slaves shipped directly from Africa to the New World was probably landed on the Spanish Caribbean island of Puerto Rico in 1519; the last shipment of slaves was probably in 1867, to Cuba, which was still a Spanish colony. We will never know precisely how many slaves were embarked on the African coast, and how many were landed in the Americas, during these three and a half centuries. However, thanks to collaborative scholarship, our knowledge of every aspect of the trade has become far more exact in recent decades. Not only do we have a very robust global estimate of the numbers of transported slaves, we also know far more about where and by whom they were bought, how much was paid for them, their destinations and their resale price in the

Americas. The first, relatively straightforward, purpose of this unit is to give you an overall sense of these quantifiable dimensions of the trade.

The second, more complex, purpose is to try to explain why a transatlantic trade in African slaves arose at all. Exploring the cultural assumptions that, apparently, prohibited such a trade will give us a better idea of why Europeans opted to purchase enslaved Africans. Here we engage with the module theme of beliefs and ideologies and also consider how religious and other beliefs legitimised slavery for early modern Europeans.

The third purpose of the unit is to assess the demographic and socio-cultural impact of the slave trade on the Americas. Unfortunately, with the exception of the English-speaking mainland colonies, sources are sparse. It is impossible to know the demographic cost to sub-Saharan Africa of the export of more than 10 million slaves over three and a half centuries since there is no hard data for Africa before about 1900.

THE OVERALL DIMENSIONS OF THE ATLANTIC SLAVE TRADE

For this section you need to go to the module website and download and print an article by David Eltis (Eltis, D., 2001, 'The volume and structure of the transatlantic slave trade: a reassessment', *William and Mary Quarterly*, 3rd series, vol. 58, no 1, January, pp. 17–46). The entire issue of this journal was devoted to evaluating the digitalised data on about 27,000 slaving voyages which were published on CD-ROM in 1999 (Eltis *et al.*, 1999). This CD-ROM provides the core of *The Trans-Atlantic Slave Trade Database* (Voyages, 2008), which you can access from the Block 4 resources on the module website. The CD-ROM does not include all slaving voyages, but internal checks demonstrate that it captures the great majority. Coverage of eighteenth-century French slaving voyages is virtually complete, and of British voyages only slightly less so. There is, for example, some record for just about every slaving voyage out of Liverpool, the most important British slaving port, and many voyages generated abundant records that have been cross-tabulated. The smaller Dutch and Danish trades are also very well documented.

The major weakness of the CD-ROM is its imperfect coverage of Portuguese and Portuguese-Brazilian slave trading, although about a quarter of the data relate to Lusophone voyages and it is highly probable that more than half are included. Given the remaining gaps in the evidence, how did Eltis arrive at new global estimates of the trade? With respect to the British, French and northern European trades, where we can be sure that few voyages are omitted, he divided his aggregates by a number which compensated for missing records. Thus, slave departures on Liverpool ships are divided by 0.99, because we can be confident that only 1 per cent of voyages from this port went unrecorded. With respect to the Lusophone trade, Eltis reworked previous estimates, using the better-documented data on imports into the English Caribbean as a check on his pre-1700 totals, for which voyage data are sparse. For example, the number of sugar plantation slaves imported into Brazil between 1600 and 1624, when Brazilian sugar exports reached their peak, is most unlikely to have exceeded the 140,000 imports into the English Caribbean between 1640 and 1675, at which latter date sugar exports from the English West Indies surpassed the level of Brazilian exports in 1624. The technology of sugar production in Brazil and the West Indies was identical, so it would have taken the same number of slaves to produce the same amount of sugar.

Now, in order to be able to complete the exercises in this section, you need to read quickly through the Eltis article. The text of the article is quite dense and it is not necessary for you to absorb every detail, but you should note how the article is structured, the main points Eltis is making and how the text relates to the tables at the end.

| EXERCISE |

Turn to Table I at the end of Eltis's article and consider how the number of slaves shipped by all nations changed over time. What does the table reveal?

Spend about 15 minutes on this exercise.

| SPECIMEN ANSWER |

First, the table shows the trade's long, gradual take off: up to the later seventeenth century, the annual flow of exports was no greater than during the post-1850 phase when a considerable international effort was being put into suppressing the trade. Second, it indicates that demand for slaves reached a plateau in the later eighteenth century: for fifty years, on average, more than 76,000 slaves were exported annually. Third, the table refutes the common misapprehension that the trade rapidly declined after Britain and the USA outlawed it: average annual exports were much higher between 1800 and 1850 than between 1700 and 1750. Slave trading continued as steamers began crossing the Atlantic and the first telegraph cables were being laid between Europe and the Americas.

| EXERCISE |

Now use the tables in Eltis to answer the following questions:

1   Which nation's traders carried the largest number of slaves to the Americas?

2   What proportions of total slave shipments were carried in British vessels between 1601 and 1650, and between 1651 and 1700? What does this indicate about the changing pattern of demand for slaves?

3   Spain had the largest land empire ever known in the Americas, which was the most important market for African slaves before 1650, and Spain was a great naval power, yet Spanish vessels shipped scarcely any slaves before the nineteenth century; why was this? (Refer also to p. 23, footnote 25, in the Eltis article.)

4   Which American region received the largest proportion of slaves throughout the trade?

5   Which was the single most important destination for slaves in the later eighteenth century?

6   What were the mortality rates on the 'Middle Passage' during the periods 1601–50, 1701–25 and 1776–1800? What do the figures imply about conditions on slave ships?

7   What proportion of slaves was shipped on British vessels between 1726 and 1800?

8   What was the principal effect of the British/US decision to outlaw the trade in 1807? What do the figures tell us about the British Navy's campaign to suppress the trade? (Look at the 'Africa' column in Part 2 of Table III, which represents the numbers of slaves liberated from slaving vessels and landed mainly in the British colony of Sierra Leone.)

9   What proportion of slave ship shipments came from West Central Africa before 1650 and between 1801 and 1850?

10   Looking at Table III, you will observe that about three times as many slaves were shipped to Jamaica as to British North America (the USA after 1776). Yet the USA had the largest slave population in the Americas by 1825. How can we explain this anomaly?

Spend about 90 minutes on this exercise.

SPECIMEN ANSWER

1   Portuguese or Portuguese-Brazilian traders shipped the largest number of slaves (over 5 million or 45.9 per cent of the total).

2   British vessels shipped 4.6 per cent of the total across the Atlantic between 1601 and 1650, and 47.8 per cent of *a far greater total* between 1651 and 1700. They increased their market share ten-fold, indicating the extraordinary expansion of sugar production in Barbados and Jamaica.

3   Spanish mainland America imported 57 per cent of slaves disembarked in the New World between 1519 and 1650 (though rather few thereafter). Eltis notes that non-Spaniards could purchase licenses (or *asientos*) to import slaves, which became much sought after by rival European commercial interests.

4   Brazil imported 40.6 per cent of all slaves landed in the Americas, and south-east Brazil was by far the most important single destination over the course of the trade.

5   However, the single most important destination in the later eighteenth century was French St Domingue: between 1751 and 1800 (effectively 1791, because of the outbreak of the rebellion), its total slave imports (593,300) exceeded Jamaica's (586,200) and south-east Brazil's (457,600).

6   The mortality rate on the 'Middle Passage' was the difference in percentage terms between the number of slaves embarked in Africa and the number landed in the Americas. In 1601–50, the mortality rate was 23.5 per cent; in 1701–25, it was 14 per cent; in 1776–1800, it was 10 per cent. The figures imply that conditions on slave ships improved (though it may be that voyage times became shorter, meaning that slaves spent less time in the ships' highly infectious environment).

7   British vessels shipped 40.7 per cent of the total between 1726 and 1800 – by far the largest national 'share' in these decades.

8   The principal effect of British and US abolition was to hand a considerable commercial advantage to Portuguese and Portuguese-Brazilian slavers. It is evident that total slave exports after 1807 declined by much less than the quantities British and American vessels were shipping before abolition. The British naval patrols had only limited effect before 1850: they liberated 91,300 slaves from intercepted slaving vessels between 1826 and 1850, but in the same

period 1,398,200 slaves were landed in the Americas (over half in south-east Brazil, which was undergoing its coffee boom).

9   West Central Africa supplied 89 per cent of slave exports before 1650 and 46 per cent between 1801 and 1850.

10 The slave population of the mainland American colonies (or the USA after 1776) grew rapidly by natural increase, unlike that of Jamaica and other Caribbean islands, where the slave population would have declined without continuous imports from Africa. Some slaves reached mainland North America via the intra-American slave trade, but even allowing for indirect imports total slave arrivals there were fewer than 400,000 (see pp. 36–7 of Eltis).

You may have noticed that, in terms of the consumer market for imports in Africa, Eltis states that Africans were discriminating consumers who did not exchange slaves for worthless baubles, and there were sharp regional variations in consumer taste (pp. 31–2). To achieve economies of scale, and avoid too long a stay on the African coast, slaving captains normally concentrated on a single port of call, to which they often returned on subsequent voyages. The central paragraph on p. 32 makes clear that slave trading was a highly specialised business in which European and African traders were equal parties. Moreover, the discussion of the regional sources of slave supply on pp. 33–5 provides evidence of the slave trade's severest impact on demography and social structures in Africa. On the evidence of slave exports, the area most affected was unquestionably West Central Africa, from where slaves were exported via Luanda, Benguela and the Congo (or Zaire) estuary. Except for the late seventeenth and early eighteenth centuries, it was always the most productive source of slave exports. In his final paragraph, Eltis emphasises how the examination of the data set requires us to revise the way we normally look at the slave trade. He argues that we should stop thinking of Africans just as victims. African agency influenced the overall supply of slaves, their age and sex profiles, and imposed all kinds of costs on European traders which they would not otherwise have had to meet.

THE AFRICAN CONTEXT OF THE ATLANTIC SLAVE TRADE

When the Portuguese established regular contacts with sub-Saharan Africa, they found societies much like their own: they had a similar range of pre-industrial crafts, engaged in regular commerce and were usually organised into kingdoms, with a recognised aristocracy or elite. Except where influenced by Islam, Africans did not practise writing, build in stone, use gunpowder or (as far as we know) sail across the oceans. But they were much better equipped to maintain equal relations with Europeans than the indigenous peoples of the Caribbean or the Brazilian littoral. One reason for this is that they had not been biologically isolated from the rest of humanity (as had native Americans) and did not succumb to the devastating epidemics that swept through the American tropics. Moreover, the African disease environment was especially hostile to incomers – a point we will develop further. But it must be stressed that Africans retained the military power to confine Europeans to the coast, where they lived and died on the sufferance of African rulers. When Europeans built their coastal forts, this was normally after an exchange of 'notes' by which they recognised African sovereignty and agreed to pay a rent.

African societies also resembled European in that many of their members lived in various degrees of unfreedom. There was nothing unusual in this: bondage of some sort has been the common lot for most of history. However, sub-Saharan Africa has been unusual in the number of slaves it has exported to other world regions since antiquity. The Muslim conquest of the southern Mediterranean basin in the seventh century, and the establishment by Muslim merchants of regular trade across the Sahara and the Red Sea, gave an added impetus to the external flow of African slaves. Islam forbad the enslavement of Muslims, and imposed a religious duty on masters to convert their slaves (though a period of religious 'apprenticeship' was condoned). As 'people of the book' Christians and Jews had a tolerated place in Islam; they could be held captive for ransom, but were not usually sold as chattels. These precepts were often ignored, but they generally meant that slaves and their children were assimilated into Islamic society over time. On the other hand, there was a constant demand for slaves (not necessarily black) in the Muslim states of North Africa and the Middle East, where they were used as concubines, soldiers, administrators and domestic servants. The fact that slavery – for pagans – was a well-recognised institution, but slaves were not a self-perpetuating class, created a regular demand for imported African slaves. The fragmentary evidence makes calculating the numbers entering the Muslim trades a hazardous matter. One scholar has tentatively estimated that 4,300 slaves a year crossed the Sahara in the fifteenth century and 5,500 a year in the sixteenth, with perhaps half that number leaving annually by the Red Sea and East African coast (Austen, 1979). When the Portuguese made contact with the Guinea states, such as Benin (see Figure 14.1) they were already integrated into Muslim slave-trading networks, and slaves were used locally as porters, to clear the forest and to mine gold. Some of the first slave trading undertaken by the Portuguese was shipping slaves from one part of the West African coast to another, where they were exchanged for gold.

EXERCISE

It has been argued that these pre-existing Muslim networks facilitated the origins and development of the transatlantic trade because West Africans were already familiarised with slave dealing. Bearing in mind the discussion in the previous section, how significant do you think the 'Muslim factor' was in the development of the transatlantic trade up to 1650? (Refer back to Eltis's Table II.)

Spend about 10 minutes on this exercise.

SPECIMEN ANSWER

Its significance was probably very marginal before the later seventeenth century; until 1650, nine out ten slaves were shipped from West Central Africa, a region untouched by Islamic influence. Annual shipments from the whole Guinea coast

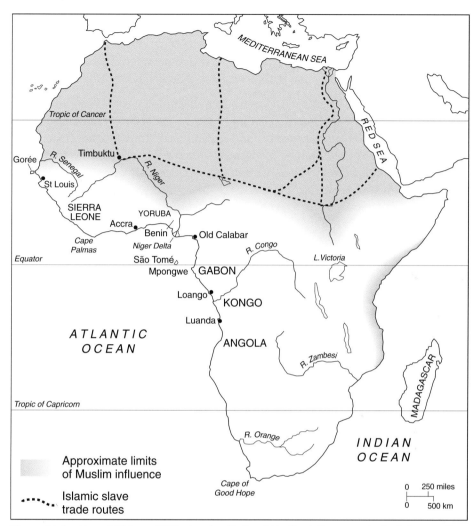

Figure 14.1   Map of Africa, *c.*1700, showing limits of Muslim influence, principal slave-trading coasts and location of places named in this unit

were less than 600 a year in the sixteenth century, and about 800 a year between 1601 and 1650.

DISCUSSION

The 'Muslim factor' was not irrelevant to the efflorescence of maritime slave trading from West Africa, but its true significance came later, in the early and mid eighteenth century, when combined exports from the Bights of Benin and Biafra, and the Gold Coast much exceeded those from West Central Africa, and the English were the main carriers. Muslim traders (known as *slatees*) supplied slaves to Europeans and Luso-Africans based on the coast, but also continued to organise trans-Saharan slave caravans. The 'Muslim factor' had a further importance in that pagans were often enslaved during jihads, or 'holy wars', in the interior, and then channelled to the coast, though again this did not become a significant way of producing slaves until the last third of the eighteenth century.

It is sometimes asked why Africans sold so many other Africans into slavery, but if you think about it this question is naive, because Africans did not *know* they were Africans before the twentieth century. This identity usually came from outside, especially from Afro-Americans travelling to Africa.

Also, sub-Saharan Africa has long been the world's most linguistically and culturally heterogeneous region. Social identities were, consequently, highly localised and focused on lineage and a community of ancestors. Household slaves were common in African societies but were rarely sold for export. So-called trade slaves were 'outsiders', usually taken in war or kidnapped by raiding parties. Figures 14.2–14.4 show various aspects of the slave trade in Africa.

Why were powerful Africans, living far beyond the influence of Islam, willing to supply trade slaves? In the academic literature, answers to that question fall into two broad positions:

- powerful Africans were seduced into supplying slaves by an external demand (the Atlantic trade), which led to the institutionalisation of slavery in African societies and the destructive extension of slave trading
- powerful Africans enhanced their wealth and power by adapting pre-existing African institutions to an external demand, which did not radically alter social structures and practices.

Figure 14.2   A coffle or human chain of slaves in the African interior. Photo: Nancy Carter/North Wind Picture Archives

Figure 14.3 Slaves being delivered by canoe to slaving vessels. Reproduced with permission of the Hakluyt Society

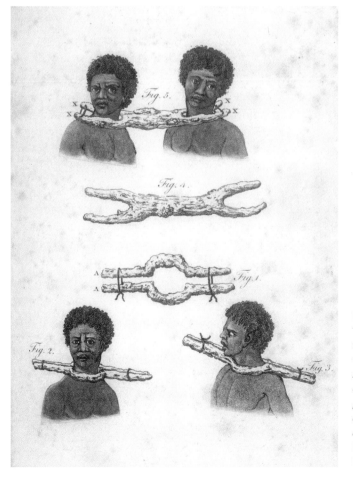

Figure 14.4 Yokes used to collar recalcitrant slaves, from Thomas Clarkson, *Letters on the slave-trade, and the state of the natives in those parts of Africa, which are contiguous to Fort St Louis and Goree*, London, James Phillips, 1791. Photo: The British Library

The first was trenchantly argued by the Guyanese Marxist Walter Rodney and popularised in *How Europe Underdeveloped Africa* (Rodney, 1972), one of the most widely read introductions to African history. In brief, Rodney argued that African societies were relatively egalitarian before contact with European slave traders. The basic unit of social organisation was the lineage and, while it included bonded subordinates and coerced dependents, it precluded a sharp division between a class of slaves and slave owners because dependents or their children were incorporated into the lineage over time. According to Rodney, external demand for human labour induced powerful Africans to turn dependents, especially those recently acquired through war, into commodities, which they exchanged for goods that either brought greater prestige (such as sumptuous Indian cottons) or more power (such as firearms and cutlasses). This led, he argued, to vicious and socially debilitating cycles of violence during which powerful Africans systematically raided enemies for slaves. It also, he believed, made the social condition of a 'trade slave' quite distinct from that of a household dependent, and so institutionalised slavery in Africa. Rodney's claims were made within the broader thesis that Europe's pre-colonial commercial relations with Africa systematically 'underdeveloped' the continent by:

- exacerbating technological backwardness (since the availability of slave labour discouraged the adoption of labour-saving technology)
- blocking capitalist development (since there was no inducement to employ wage labour and profit from rising labour productivity)
- fostering political fragmentation.

These were powerful arguments but with respect to the question asked – why were powerful Africans willing to supply trade slaves? – the balance of academic opinion has shifted to the second position. Historians are now much more insistent on the primacy of African agency in the slave trade. John Thornton put the case very clearly in *Africa and Africans in the Making of the Atlantic World, 1400–1680*:

> the slave trade ... should not be seen as an 'impact' brought in from outside and functioning as some sort of autonomous factor in African history. Instead, it grew out of and was rationalized by the African societies who participated in it and had complete control over it until the slaves were loaded onto European ships for transfer to Atlantic societies.

> The reason that slavery was widespread in Africa was not ... because Africa was an economically underdeveloped region in which forced labor had not yet been replaced by free labor. Instead, slavery was rooted in deep-seated legal and institutional structures of African societies, and it functioned quite differently from the way it functioned in European societies.

Slavery was widespread in Atlantic Africa [before contact with Europeans] because slaves were the only form of private, revenue-producing property recognized in African law. By contrast, in European legal systems, land was the primary form of private, revenue-producing property, and slavery was relatively minor ... [African] slavery was in many ways the functional equivalent of the landlord–tenant relationship in Europe and was perhaps as widespread.

Thus, it was the absence of landed private property – or, to be more precise, it was the corporate ownership of land – that made slavery so pervasive an aspect of African society ... [it] was possibly the most important avenue for private, reproducing wealth available to Africans [and] it is hardly surprising that it should have been so widespread and, moreover, be a good indicator of the most dynamic segments of African society, where private initiative was operating most freely.

(Thornton, 1992, pp. 74, 86)

EXERCISE

We look to evidence to settle historical arguments and, while we have none emanating directly from African societies, we have a fair amount from Europeans with first-hand knowledge of slaving. Much of it was compiled as the abolition movement gathered momentum in Britain in the later 1780s and the trade's impact on African societies became a matter of public controversy. Thomas Clarkson, who led the movement outside parliament, was indefatigable in gathering testimony from men who had served on slaving ships, which he published as *Essay on the Efficiency of Regulation of Abolition* (1789). But the trade's defenders were just as energetic in presenting testimony to support their interests, and found some highly congenial opinions in a series of letters from Sierra Leone by John Matthews, a Royal Navy lieutenant, who served there in 1785–87. (On his return, he was deputed by the Committee of the Liverpool African Merchants to give evidence to the committee of the Privy Council that enquired into the trade in 1788.) Extracts from Clarkson's pamphlet and Matthews's letters are reproduced as Anthology Documents 4.2 and 4.3. Read these documents, summarise their key contentions and say which gives the more persuasive account of the trade's impact on African societies. (Note: the Clarkson material consists of excerpts from his informants' journals; the 'I' is not Clarkson himself.)

Spend about 1 hour on this exercise.

SPECIMEN ANSWER

Matthews's key contention in his letter from Sierra Leone was that slavery was endemic in Africa and that surplus slaves were being incidentally produced by the incessant wars between 'a prodigious number of small independent states' and the routine use of enslavement as a punishment. Had the surplus slaves not been sold to Europeans they would, he maintained, have either died from starvation or been put to death. The claim that Africans in the interior would sell their wives and children for salt (mined in the Sahara) was hearsay, as was his contention that 'Death or slavery were, and still are, the punishments for almost every offence'. His letter from Liverpool was a conscious riposte to the abolition movement. In it, he emphatically denied that wars were undertaken in Africa specifically to acquire slaves or at the instigation of European traders. He noted how jihads in the interior generated a flow of slaves to the coast and was at pains to counter the abolitionists' assertion that the number of offences punishable by slavery in African societies had grown to satisfy the external demand for slaves. Matthews had no direct knowledge of the slave-supply regions in the interior and was relying on information provided by African slave merchants: the 'concurring testimony of many of the most intelligent natives' that jihadists put to death conquered people who refused to convert may have been true, but it was not something Matthews had observed. Nevertheless, Matthews was a persuasive witness who skilfully absolved Europeans from prime responsibility for the slave trade while maintaining that warfare and disruption in African societies preceded the trade and would not have been lessened without it. Though they would be loath to align themselves with Matthews, the views of many modern scholars – such as Thornton – are surprisingly close to his.

The Clarkson material contains first-hand evidence of raids conducted in the Niger Delta and the Cape Palmas region with the express intent of procuring slaves for the Atlantic trade, and more circumstantial evidence of slaving parties in Angola leaving for the interior without any trade goods, with the clear implication that they were raiding (not trading) for captives. But, in one respect, we have to take more on trust: Matthews was a naval lieutenant prepared to put his views to a committee of the Privy Council; Clarkson was publishing extracts from the journals of unnamed informants. That reservation aside, there are no compelling reasons to doubt their testimony.

DISCUSSION

So who was 'right'? Looking at the map of Africa, it is quite possible both sides were: Old Calabar is hundreds, and Angola thousands, of miles from Sierra Leone, and political and cultural conditions varied greatly from region to region. The Muslim presence in the hinterland of Sierra Leone unquestionably brought the jihad into play as a slave-supply mechanism; the Angolan slaving frontier was peculiarly desolate because people migrated inland to escape slaving parties. One conclusion to draw from this exercise is that abolition was not an easy victory for 'progressive' opinion. In refusing to see Africans merely as victims and in stressing that their initiative and enterprise were essential to the trade, today's historians show an affinity with its European defenders rather than its opponents.

THE EUROPEAN CONTEXT OF THE ATLANTIC SLAVE TRADE

Beliefs and ideologies

While the primary purpose of New World slavery was to extract an economic profit, it was not a 'purely' economic system. Had it been so, white slaves would have toiled alongside blacks. Europeans had in the past enslaved other Europeans; indeed, our word slave is derived from Slav, after the ethnic origins of the Caucasian slaves supplied to the Italian cities by Genoese traders from their colonies on the Black Sea. In the ancient world prisoners of war generally became slaves. Indeed, early modern Europeans had little compunction about working other Europeans to death in *punitive* slavery. Tens, perhaps hundreds, of thousands convicted of non-capital offences were condemned for life to Mediterranean galley slavery. Such was the demand for galley labour that German states regularly sold convicted criminals to Mediterranean ports. Irish and Catholic rebels defeated in the seventeenth-century British Civil Wars were sold as slaves to Barbadian planters. The poor who could, but did not, labour were stigmatised and criminalised throughout Europe: convicted vagrants could be whipped, mutilated and forced to work in houses of correction. For the labouring poor, notions of civil liberty were selective, even in the more liberal states: British sailors were kidnapped by state agents and forced into the Royal Navy. Until the later eighteenth century, Scottish miners were serfs; when a mine changed hands, they were sold along with the winding gear and mineral rights. However, the Europeans who founded West Indian and American plantation colonies never contemplated enslaving whites as chattel slaves. The fact that New World slaves were, barring tiny numbers of Native Americans, exclusively coerced black migrants alerts us to the beliefs and ideologies that shaped the plantation system from its inception.

Here we have to refer to a backdrop of cultural assumptions which in the later Middle Ages had led, at least in northern Europe, to all white Christians being included within an implicit community of those who could not be bought and sold as slaves, however barbarously they might be treated in other ways. The distinction between punitive and chattel slavery had become very clear in law and custom, and the latter had virtually disappeared from northern Europe by about 1400. The enslavement of defeated enemies was sanctioned by the Roman 'law of nations' but this could justify neither the enslavement of the king's peaceful subjects, nor slavery being a hereditary condition for people who, in natural law, were regarded as 'born free'. The basis of this implicit community was ethnicity rather than religion: Catholicism and orthodoxy had condoned slavery for a millennium and more. Theologians could cite unambiguous scriptural authority for hereditary slavery for 'outsiders', which many saw as punishment for original sin. Baptism did not redeem a black skin from slavery.

Before they began to ship Africans across the Atlantic in great numbers, Europeans entertained various beliefs and prejudices as to why black people should not be part of their implicit community. Their bible was the most authoritative source for all belief; in Genesis, they found an account both of humankind's common origins but also of ethnic differences within the human family, which could be traced to the sons of Noah. Ham was the second son who saw his drunken father, naked and asleep. When Noah awoke and realised his humiliation, he cursed, not Ham, but Ham's son Canaan: 'a servant of servants shall he be unto his brethren'. Where the Canaanites multiplied – and note they were denizens of Sodom and Gomorrah, among other unsavoury places – then 'These are the sons of Ham, after their families, after their tongues ... and in their *nations*' (Genesis 10.20, emphasis added). The translators of the King James Bible used 'nation' insistently in Genesis: it conveyed the idea of where you were born and from whom you were descended; the closest modern usage would be ethnicity. The Bible does not say that the 'nations' of Ham are black, but the genealogies and apocryphal interpolations imply that they migrated into lands, notably Ethiopia, which indubitably came to be inhabited by black people. The dark skinned were often referred to as Hamites or Chamites, who bore the curse of Canaan. Although to us cursing children for the sins of their fathers is a monstrous injustice, it was taken as God's inscrutable purpose if you believed the Bible is his word and reveals his mind. So its literal reading could sanction the notion that black people were divinely ordained for perpetual servitude.

The rediscovery of the classical heritage allowed Europeans to link religious dogma to an intellectual rationale for black slavery. Aristotle had asserted that barbarians were slaves by nature and conceived of slavery as the natural relationship of superior and inferior within a household, qualitatively the same as the natural relation of father to child, man to wife, mind to body. The rational basis for slavery lay in the slave's innate, natural inferiority. Aristotle did not say that black people were naturally inferior, and therefore slavish, but blacks had no writing, and indulged in barbarous practices such as polygamy, human sacrifice and selling their own people as slaves. The reclamation of Aristotle's thought encouraged Europeans to pin the idea that some were slaves by nature onto Africans or Hamites.

This is not to say that a racist, quasi-Aristotelian rationale for black slavery had been elaborated before the great acceleration of the trade in the late seventeenth century. Such a rationale was to come later, in the writings of men like Edward Long, the historian of Jamaica, who appears in 'Sugar dynasty' on DVD 2. But there was a clustering of beliefs and ideologies that made black servitude untroubling for white Europeans. As far as possible we must avoid invoking hindsight and applying our standards and morality to the past we are studying. For example, racism is a clearly defined concept in western societies today enshrined in law, but in the eighteenth century no such ideas about racism had yet been formulated or legally defined.

Commercial organisation

Let us turn from beliefs to the business history of slave trading, which reflected broader changes in the commercial organisation of early modern capitalism. The slave trade was initially conducted through the commercial policies and practices that historians have called mercantilism. Mercantilism referred to the measures early modern states took to ensure a favourable balance of international trade. It was recognised that trade between sovereign states could be mutually advantageous: Britain and Portugal, for example, concluded the Methuen Treaty in 1703 by which the Portuguese agreed to admit British woollens and the British agreed to admit Portuguese wines at preferential rates. But colonial trade was a branch of international commerce in which the state could use its sovereign power to exclude foreigners and to compel its colonists to trade only with the mother country. By reserving the trade for the mother country, states could avoid competition. In the interests of promoting metropolitan economic interests, most states forbad manufacturing and processing in their colonies: sugar could only be exported from the British Caribbean in an unrefined state, for example. The slave trade and plantation slavery were embedded in mercantilist regulations intended to augment the sovereign state's economic power.

Mercantilism

Mercantilism is a historians' term for the regulatory economic systems introduced by early modern states to ensure a positive balance of payments. It usually involved a national monopoly on colonial trade and tariff discrimination against foreign vessels, as well as the absolute ban on importing certain manufactures to protect domestic producers. It was recognised, though, that trade between sovereign states could be advantageous. Thus, the key idea was that trade was a zero-sum game; that is, that a country could accumulate wealth through a balance of trade surplus only at the expense of another country. By the mid eighteenth century, mercantilism was challenged by a number of political economists, including Adam Smith, who promoted free trade, and was widely discredited as an economic theory.

Around 1650, the leading players in the slave trade were national chartered corporations with a monopoly on the Africa trade and on purchasing and shipping African slaves to their respective colonies. Mercantilist states delegated sovereign powers to these companies: they could enter treaties with African potentates, build forts to protect themselves against other Europeans, and even wage war. The companies maintained factors, slave-holding pens and small military establishments on the African coast, and conducted what was called 'castle trade'. The British monopoly was transferred from an earlier chartered company to the Royal African Company in 1672 and was supposed to last for a thousand years. But 'private' interlopers were coming into the trade by 1690, and the monopoly was formally ended in 1698 when the trade was opened to all merchants in the British empire on payment to the company of a 10 per cent duty on exports to Africa. This Ten Per Cent Act expired in 1712 when the last remnant of crown control of Britain's Africa trade ended. The company retained responsibility for its forts and factors in the Gambia and along the Gold Coast and Slave Coast (for which it received a state subsidy) but henceforth the African trade was an open market dominated by private merchants. When the company was chartered, the value of African commodity exports (principally gold) had been roughly equal to the value of slave exports. As the move to private trade gathered momentum, the relative value of African commodity exports declined: the Africa trade became virtually synonymous with the slave trade.

Elsewhere, the shift from monopoly trade to competitive trading by private partnerships came rather later. In France, the slave trade was opened to independent merchants in 1716, with the exception of trade with the colonial ports of St Louis and Gorée (see Figure 14.1), where the chartered Compagnie du Sénégal retained its monopoly for most of the eighteenth century. In both countries, the great majority of slaving partnerships owned the vessel as well as the cargo. Occasionally, a slaving partnership would have a resident factor on the African coast, but more usually they employed a 'supercargo' aboard the slaving vessel to oversee the transactions and protect their interests. Private slavers engaged in 'coasting trade', although, as you will have gathered from Eltis, they usually concentrated on one port of call. Slaving captains worked on commission, which was typically a percentage of the slave cargo. French business partnerships were almost invariably family based and, from around 1750, the leading slavers were predominantly from Protestant and Jewish families, based in Nantes and Le Havre. The most successful were among the richest families in the realm, able to buy prestigious public offices and patents of nobility (Stein, 1979, p. 188).

One of the intriguing findings from the slave-trade database is that, both during the monopoly period and after the switch to wholly private trade, British ships carried 50 per cent more slaves per ton and twice as many slaves per crew member than their French counterparts (Eltis, 2000, p. 123) (see Figures 14.5 and 14.6). This gave British slavers a considerable competitive edge because shipping costs (made up of sailors' wages and subsistence, the captain's commission, insurance and capital replacement costs) accounted for about three-quarters of the final price of a slave. Delivering European and Asian exports to Africa doubled their price on the African coast, and delivering slaves to the Americas doubled their price. Behind the splendid productivity record of British vessels lay incalculable misery, since the conditions endured by slaves on the Middle Passage were far more wretched than those imposed on convicts. A slave ship carried three times as many coerced passengers as a convict ship of comparable tonnage. Voyages from Africa to the Americas averaged about three months; had they lasted a year, and sustained the same mortality rates, they would have been as lethal to the slaves and crew as the Black Death.

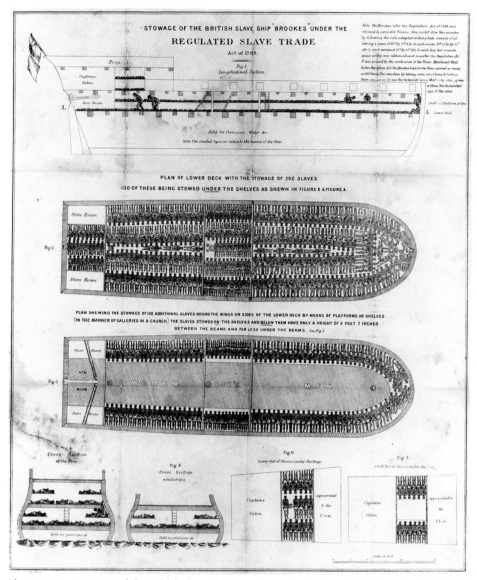

Figure 14.5   Stowage of the British slave ship *Brookes* under the Regulated Slave Trade Act of 1788, broadside, *c*.1790. Photo: Library of Congress. The infamous conditions on British slaving vessels were publicised in 1788 by the abolitionist movement when it circulated the plan of *The Brookes*. We can compare this with the plan of the French slave ship *L'Aurore* (Figure 14.6), drawn about the same time. Interestingly, there seems to have been more space to reach the slaves on *L'Aurore*; whether this was because the French drawing was more realistic – as some have suggested – or whether *The Brookes* really did fill every inch with slaves is a moot point

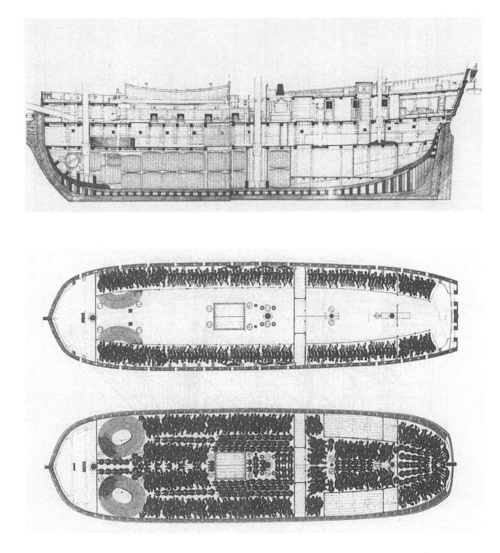

Figure 14.6   Plan of the French slave ship *L'Aurore*. Reproduced with permission of Archéologie Navale Classique Recherche Édition (ANCRE)

EXERCISE

Using Table 14.1, write a paragraph summarising the changes in the geographic location of the British end of the trade; how would you account for these changes?

Table 14.1   Clearances of slave ships from British ports, 1699–1807

	London	Bristol	Liverpool	Newport	Other (includes colonial ports)	Total
1699–1729	1,595	586	173	12	217	2,583
1730–1749	363	644	553	118	134	1,812
1750–1779	869	624	1,949	358	456	4,256
1780–1807	524	251	2,524	–	153	3,452
1699–1807	3,351	2,105	5,199	488	960	12,103

(Source: derived from Richardson, 1998, p. 446)

SPECIMEN ANSWER

In the early eighteenth century, the British trade was predominantly in the hands of London-based merchants, but after 1730 it shifted to west of England ports, presumably because they had a geographic advantage. Vessels sailing out of London were often delayed by adverse winds in the English Channel, and so took longer to reach Africa. Bristol was briefly the most important slaving port, but around 1750 it was overtaken by Liverpool, from which the great majority of slaving vessels departed in the trade's final decades. The reasons for the shift to the Mersey are not wholly clear, but proximity to Lancashire's developing cotton industry may have been a factor, since textiles were normally the major item in a ship's cargo.

DISCUSSION

London's financial community was vital in furnishing credit at the outset of the trade and continued to have this role even after its relocation to Bristol and Liverpool. The planters or planters' agents who bought slaves in the Americas very rarely did so for cash; they signed a bill of exchange (a written order requiring them to make payment at a later specified date) in favour of their slave suppliers, which would mature in twelve to twenty-four months, and which London finance houses would guarantee (for a discount). This bill would return to, say, Liverpool, where the slaving partnership used it to settle accounts with *their* suppliers, or re-invested it in further voyages. The planter honoured his debt to the London finance house when his sugar harvest was marketed in Britain, and so obtained further credit. London merchants were also major suppliers of the trade goods supplied on credit to Bristol and Liverpool slavers, partly because London remained the hub of the more lucrative East India trade. Indian textiles and cowrie shells – which were used as money in West Africa – were important in the Africa trade's export schedule.

A commercial system so dependent on medium-term credit required the legal state to impose stiff penalties on those defaulting on their bonds. Until the 1730s, debt recovery in the British slave empire was hampered by the contradictory interests of two jurisdictions: the colonial assemblies were planter-dominated and sought, therefore, a legal regime favourable to debtors. London and provincial merchants were represented in the

Westminster parliament, so it was more sympathetic to creditors. The crucial bone of contention between the jurisdictions was whether real estate and fixed capital could be seized in payment of a planter's debt or whether, as in Brazil and the French colonies, these productive assets were protected against seizure. (A Brazilian or French creditor foreclosing on an indebted planter could seize his harvest, money and personal effects, but not his land and mill, nor his slaves.) The metropolitan merchants eventually persuaded parliament to pass the Colonial Debts Act of 1732, which imposed a uniform debt regime on the British American colonies, and declared that the 'lands, houses, chattels, and slaves' of colonial debtors were liable for the satisfaction of debts 'in the like Manner as Real Estates are by the Law of England liable to Satisfaction of Debts due by Bond or other Specialty' (quoted in Price, 1991, p. 309). When the law was passed, sugar prices were at an all-time low, and many planters were in financial trouble. The law gave metropolitan merchants the confidence they needed to extend their credit operations and, though bitterly denounced by colonial planters, benefited them in the long run. The English-speaking Atlantic developed credit networks of unrivalled efficiency, which gave planters access to far more working capital than was available to planters in other slave empires. The law also underlined the negation of the slaves' human rights; since they could be seized and sold in satisfaction of their owners' debts, it gave legal sanction to the break up of slave families (which was forbidden under the French *Code Noir* or slave code).

The trade had solid social foundations because its risks and profits were spread among many partners and investors. It was not, as in France, the business of exclusive family networks. A core of ship owners emerged who managed the trade, while 'passive' investors provided much of the working capital. Slave ships were smaller than in other national trades and voyages were cheaper to fit out. The annual returns on slave-trading voyages after about 1750 averaged around 8–10 per cent, which was higher than in domestic commerce, but the risks were much greater: a slave cargo could be wiped out by disease; ship-board revolts were not uncommon; ships could be seized by privateers in time of war. And with voyages taking up to eighteen months to complete, there was a delay in realising one's investment. Nevertheless, capital was raised without any apparent difficulty; about £200,000 was invested annually in the Liverpool slave trade around 1750 and probably more than £1 million in 1800.

We noted earlier that slave trading on the African coast had to conform to the regional preferences of African consumers, so cargoes varied somewhat between national trades and even ports. Portuguese slavers invariably traded directly between Brazil and Africa, so Brazilian produce – roll tobacco and *aguardente*, a sugar brandy – made up a significant proportion of their shipments. Similarly, when Rhode Island slavers entered the trade, they specialised in shipping rum. But British and French traders tended to ship similar cargoes of mixed manufactures in which textiles were the largest single item. Textiles represented 59 per cent by value of all goods shipped to Africa from France in 1775 and 64 per cent in 1788, but nearly all these cloth exports were produced in India – a telling reflection of economic globalisation in this era. The next most important item in the French export schedule was brandy, which constituted about 10 per cent of exports (Klein, 1990, p. 291). Although the Asian component was exceptionally high in France's Africa trade, the relative weights of its exports was representative of all Atlantic trade with Africa.

Whether the trade was as socially destructive as its critics claimed is debatable. Much turns on the frequency with which the exchange of guns and gunpowder for slaves exacerbated cycles of social violence. During the 1780s – the trade's peak decade – guns and gunpowder were less than 10 per cent of imports by value (Eltis, 1991). Knowing the price of guns, and making heroic assumptions about western Africa's population, we can hazard that one gun per 118 persons was being imported, which suggests they had a restricted role in diffusing social violence. Undeniably, enslavement was a violent process, but many kidnappers and coffle guards were armed with traditional weapons.

AFRICAN TRADE

This section will focus on the commercial arrangements between African and European slave traders. The issues discussed here help historians understand how trade was organised and perpetuated. Traders exchanged goods, and for African traders the 'goods' they exchanged for European goods were slaves. As you learned earlier in this unit, Africans acquired slaves through various means and those that did so can be identified as 'producers', just as we might talk of coffee or cocoa 'producers'. What was being 'produced' and then sold here was labour, the labour potential of human beings, to be utilised in the sugar growing and production processes in the New World. To view the slave trade in such stark commercial terms highlights its inhumanity; nevertheless, this is how traders are likely to have viewed it.

Did African slave traders receive a 'fair price' for their slaves? Morally, this is an absurd question. Even economically it doesn't make much sense, since the social costs of exporting Africa's scarcest productive asset, its people, must in the long run have wiped out private gains. By selling labour, powerful Africans made their societies, and themselves, poorer over time. But in the objective analysis of the slave market system it is a highly relevant question. We tend to assume that trade between industrialised (or industrialising) countries and non-industrialised ones, particularly in the tropical world, is unfair, with the former exploiting the latter. But, as we have seen, Africans had considerable control over the slave trade in Africa and it appears that this extended to the 'price' they gained for their slaves. Issues of supply and demand affected this market as they would any other. A major item that Africans exchanged for slaves with British traders was textiles and evidence shows that African merchants exploited the fluctuations in textile prices. For example, textile imports into Africa became relatively cheaper in the early nineteenth century because of increased productivity in the industrialising world. Consequently, African merchants could command more imported cloth for a slave in 1820 than they could in 1800 and more in 1840 than in 1820.

As you have seen, contemporary records are available showing the numbers of slaves shipped across the Atlantic and sold in the New World, but calculating the 'prices' paid for slaves by European traders is much more difficult. One reason for this is that traders from Europe mostly bartered goods such as textiles for slaves rather than paying for them in a recognised currency. Thus the best source for constructing a series of slave prices in Africa is the value of the goods to be exchanged for slaves when ships were loaded at European ports. Excise officials valued the cargoes and from their records we can establish the *prime cost* of the average slave (i.e. the cost before any expenses are added). We use 'prime cost' here because we are dealing with the value of the goods as they are loaded onto the ship. The actual cost of a slave purchase included the additional costs of transporting the trade goods to Africa and insuring them in transit. To further complicate things, in the British case, eighteenth-century excise records were kept in 'official' values, based on prices prevailing in 1696–1700, which diverged from market prices as the century progressed. In effect, they are in constant prices which indicate trends in volume rather than the actual prices ('current prices') of British exports to Africa. This can be useful in gauging changes in the barter terms between Africans and Europeans.

Using the method outlined above, David Richardson compiled a price series for slaves essentially by comparing the estimated number of slaves shipped by British slave traders from the African coast year by year in the eighteenth century with the annual value of the exports to Africa. Richardson stresses the difficulty of compiling such a price series due to the unreliability of the data and so we must take this as only one historian's assessment, although it does to some degree corroborate findings by other historians (Richardson, 1991, pp. 24, 33).

Richardson calculated that the prime price of an average slave rose from about £5 in 1698 to £29–£35 in money terms by the 1800s, and from £5 to £23–£29 in real terms (i.e. adjusted for inflation). However, prices did not increase steadily over time: they fluctuated between £4 and £6 up to 1740, rose gently to about £7 in the next two decades, and then doubled between the 1760s and outbreak of the American War of Independence (1775–83). After being checked by the war, prices rose again in the later 1780s, reached a plateau in the early 1790s, and then surged ahead in the final years of the British trade (Richardson, 1991, p. 33).

As these figures suggest, European slave traders could not entirely dictate the 'price' they paid for slaves. In the first half of the eighteenth century, the cost of goods bartered for slaves needed to rise only a little to expand the supply of slaves. At this time Europeans could obtain a sufficient supply of slaves without having to offer a higher price in most years; some 2,269,000 were sold over fifty years at static prices. But over the next fifty years demand increased and 3,826,000 slaves were sold (a 69 per cent increase in supply) and real prices rose more than three-and-a-half-fold to elicit this supply. Thus, as demand increased, material inducements to export slaves had to be stepped up, with the implication that coercion within Africa rose to unprecedented levels to overcome supply 'bottlenecks'. Prices apparently became really high in the 1800s, as planters sought to replenish their stock while the trade was still legal.

From Table 14.2, you will see that Richardson's price series correlates closely with price movements for slaves in Jamaica. Given that most of the African coast was an open market, we can be sure other national traders were paying the high prices demanded in the final years of the British trade. The St Domingue revolution and the French decree of 1794 abolishing slavery (listed in the chronology on the A200 website) removed one competitor for slaves, but the British faced others: US slavers were rushing to stock up while federal law still permitted slave imports; Spanish slavers were beginning to supply the Cuban sugar planters; the Portuguese were servicing Brazil's resurgent plantations. With St Domingue in ruins, Brazil's sugar exports soared in the 1790s and 1800s, while planters also invested in a new slave crop, namely cotton. Between 1798 and 1807, about 60,000 African slaves arrived at Salvador in Bahia (Schwartz, 1987, p. 351). African slave entrepreneurs dominated a seller's market, where demand was high.

Table 14.2   Current prices of slaves in Africa and the Caribbean: 1700–1806

	Average current price of a slave in Africa (£) (5-year moving average, except 1806)	Average current price of a prime male slave sold in Jamaica (£) (5-year moving average, except 1806)
1701	5.1	24
1725	5.7	24
1750	6.4	32.6
1775	15.2	49
1800	27.3	78.7
1806	41.1	82.9

(Sources: Richardson, 1991; Eltis and Richardson, 2004)

THE DEMOGRAPHIC CONSEQUENCES OF THE SLAVE TRADE IN THE NEW WORLD

The European discovery and conquest of the Americas triggered the most momentous demographic upheavals in history. The population declined precipitously in the densely populated highlands and was virtually annihilated in the lowland tropics. Apart from 500 or so Caribs in Dominica, who mostly possess West African genes through interbreeding with escaped slaves, and a few people of predominantly native descent in Cuba and Puerto Rico, nothing now remains of the indigenous Caribbean peoples (Watts, 1987, p. 41). Native Brazilians fared almost as badly, and with them died one potential labour supply.

The migratory response to this demographic catastrophe was unique in the history of human migrations for two reasons: first, before 1820, four out of every five migrants to the Americas were either slaves or indentured servants and so sailed with the expectation of being in some form of servitude after the voyage; second, the great majority came not from the continent and states that had seized political control of the New World, but from Africa. Three out every four people who migrated across the Atlantic before 1820 were African slaves. At the slave trade's apogee, between 1760 and 1820, the ratio of African to European migrants was almost six to one; the influx of *permanent* white migrants did not surpass slave imports until 1840. For this reason, Afro-Americans have deeper historical roots in the modern United States than do white Americans: the median date for the arrival of the ancestors of present-day black US citizens was about 1770; the median date for the arrival of the ancestors of present-day Euro-America citizens was about 1900 (Curtin, 1990, p. 109). Prior to the great European migrations of the mid and later nineteenth century, nothing could be more mistaken than the ideological association between the New World and Europeans striving for freedom.

In Britain, we can be forgiven for making that association because English-speaking peoples had an exceptional propensity to migrate during the seventeenth century – when political liberties were being fiercely contested – and the colonies they founded in temperate North America were the world's freest political communities, though one must add 'for whites'. But temperate North America was not the focus of European expansion in the New World. Europeans located most of their capital, and concentrated most labour (whether native or imported), first in the mining economies of Mexico and Peru, and then in the plantation economies of the tropical and subtropical lowlands. The temperate New England colonies were an economic backwater, where the net worth of free white people was, on average, only a quarter of the net worth of whites in the colonies of the upper and lower south. The New England colonists secured a modest prosperity only when they began producing food and other supplies for the plantation islands; by about 1760, three-quarters of their exports were going to the British West Indies (Solow, 1991a, p. 30). The most rapid development in the thirteen colonies (Figure 14.7) occurred where an export crop could be produced by coerced labour. Initially, this had been tobacco, grown by white indentured workers. But tobacco was also being grown in Europe (including England), and the Virginia planters only came to dominate the market by turning to black slaves. Supplementary slave-grown exports were rice and indigo, mainly from Carolina. However, around 1770, the exports of a few West Indian islands were worth more than the total exports of the mainland colonies *combined*, despite their abundant fertile land, their forests of valuable timber and navigable rivers, their herds of European cattle and horses, and their fecund white settlers (see Table 14.3).

Figure 14.7 The thirteen mainland colonies in 1776

Table 14.3   The annual average exports of British North America, 1768–72

	Total exports (£m)	Percentage produced by slave labour	Percentage exported to slave colonies
West Indies	3,910.6	Nearly 100	
Upper south	1,046.9	*c.*50	
Lower south	551.9	*c.*75	
Middle colonies	526.5		42
New England	439.1		78
Total	6,475.0		

(Source: Solow, 1991a, p. 29)

Whatever jurisdiction they were under, the tropical and sub-tropical plantation economies only prospered through the 'blackening' of the labour force and the intensification of servitude (see Table 14.4). Black slaves came to greatly outnumber whites and freed people and their labour-force participation rate was the highest the world has known in peacetime. New World slave populations had very few 'economic dependents', with virtually none of the age and gender differences evident among the free. African women were set to tasks rarely undertaken by white women, certainly in north-western Europe. Planters quickly suppressed any culturally bound scruples about deploying female slaves outside the household and were gender blind when organising whip-driven gang labour. The proportion of children who could not be made to

Table 14.4   Slaves, whites and freed people in New World populations at selected dates

	White	Freed	Slave	Slave : white ratio
Barbados, 1690	20,000	–	60,000	3.00 : 1
Barbados, 1833	12,797	6,584	80,861	6.32 : 1
Jamaica, 1698	7,400	–	40,000	5.41 : 1
Jamaica, 1834	15,000	35,000	310,000	20.67 : 1
St Domingue, 1681	4,336	–	2,312	0.53 : 1
St Domingue, 1791	30,381	24,000	480,000	15.8 : 1
Cuba, 1774	96,440	30,847	44,333	0.46 : 1
Cuba, 1827	311,051	106,494	286,942	0.92 : 1
USA, 1780	2,204,949	28,771	546,649	0.25 : 1
USA, 1830	12,858,670	319,599	2,009,043	0.16 : 1
USA, 1860	31,443,008	488,070	3,953,760	0.13 : 1

work was also low, partly because male slave imports exceeded female by a ratio of about three to two, but chiefly because of devastating infant mortality. The labour productivity of New World slave populations – or the amount of marketable produce produced per person per year – far outstripped that of non-slave populations in Europe.

If you refer back to Tables II and III in the Eltis article that you downloaded, you will observe that the total number of slaves entering Barbados, Jamaica and St Domingue greatly exceeded their slave and free populations in the 1830s (or, in St Domingue's case, 1791). The combined black and freed population of Barbados was less than 90,000, although nearly half a million slaves had been shipped to the island in the previous one and half centuries. Some of this discrepancy can be explained by intra-American shipments of slaves, but its principal cause was a chronic excess of deaths over births in slave populations in the tropics and semi-tropics. On the sugar plantations, death triumphed over life: the intense exploitation of labour, poor diet and the disease environment negated humankind's elementary compulsion to reproduce its own. The records of one Barbadian estate show that, between 1712 and 1748, 5 per cent of its labour force of 238 slaves had to be replaced each year (Watts, 1987, p. 366). Without continuous slave imports from Africa, sugar island populations would have decreased by a rate varying from 10 per thousand annually up to 40 per thousand annually (Curtin, 1969, p. 28). Fresh arrivals from Africa caused the vicious cycle of demographic wastage to persist because their mortality rate was higher than that of Creole slaves and their reproduction rate low, on account of unfavourable sex ratios. Only late in the history of Caribbean slavery was the point reached where the deficit between deaths and births diminished, the proportion of American-born slaves began to grow and fresh slave imports were only needed to open 'virgin land', such as Guyana. Barbados's population stabilised around 1810, but Jamaica's did not do so until the 1840s, after slavery had ended.

EXERCISE

What impact do you think the very high price of slaves at the beginning of the nineteenth century had on their treatment in the West Indies?

Spend just a few minutes on this exercise.

SPECIMEN ANSWER

They were an incentive for planters to improve the slaves' living conditions and to encourage them to breed.

DISCUSSION

There is evidence that rising prices had precisely that effect. Even before the abolition of the trade, planters began to clothe their slaves better, engaged doctors to care for the sick and women in childbirth, and instructed overseers not to over-work pregnant slaves. To improve diets, more land was set aside for food crops. Abolition gave a further impetus to so-called amelioration as planters sought to establish a self-sustaining labour force. However, while mortality was reduced *fertility* remained low, and about half the female slaves in the British West Indies never bore a child. Several reasons have been adduced for this, including endemic venereal disease, which rendered many women sterile, and a protein deficient diet, which caused irregular ovulation. Furthermore, the planters' wish to see women slaves breed conflicted with the need to employ them in the cane fields, where they were in the majority in the labour gangs; the heavy work – normally fifteen hours a day but eighteen during the harvest – induced frequent miscarriages in the first stages of pregnancy. Added to which, post-natal mortality remained stubbornly high (Ward, 1998, pp. 429–32).

As Figure 14.8 makes clear, the historical demography of slavery in the thirteen colonies (and later the USA) was quite distinct, for there natural increase soon contributed much more to population growth than did the transatlantic trade. Around 1800, mortality rates for North American slaves were similar to rates for Jamaican slaves but their fertility was about 80 per cent higher. Had slaves in the United States duplicated the demographic experience of the British West Indies, the black population in 1800 would have been 186,000; in fact, there were 1.002 million blacks in the USA at that date. Although only 4 per cent of all slave imports were to the thirteen colonies or USA, well over a third of slaves in the western hemisphere lived in the USA in 1825 (Fogel and Engerman, 1974, p. 29).

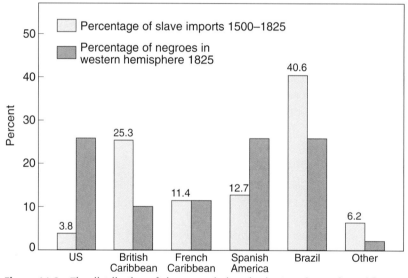

Figure 14.8   The distribution of slave populations in the Americas. Adapted from Fogel and Engerman (1974) p. 28, and Eltis *et al.* (1999)

As has been said, demographically, the Americas were an extension of Africa, not of Europe, until the early nineteenth century. Unfortunately, since there is no hard data for African demographic history before about 1900, we cannot know the demographic cost to sub-Saharan Africa of the export of more than 10 million slaves over three and a half centuries.

CONCLUSION

We have not done with the Atlantic slave trade; in a later unit you will study its abolition and suppression. But we have a reached point where we can summarise its role in the making of the modern Atlantic 'world'.

EXERCISE

To do so, make a list of how this unit relates to the themes of the module.

Spend about 20 minutes on this exercise.

DISCUSSION

Taking first the producers and consumers theme, it is clear that the slave trade and slavery were entirely economic arrangements in which, in basic terms, there were a number of producers and consumers. Europeans shipped goods to sub-Saharan Africa, which were exchanged for slaves with African merchants. Large numbers of Africans were then shipped across the Atlantic to the Americas, where they were sold for profit. The Africans then laboured as slaves on plantations, which in turn made profits for plantation owners from the goods produced. The cooperation of Africans in Africa and their acceptance of slavery as a long-established part of their culture made the Atlantic slave trade possible for Europeans. African agency was also important in ensuring that African traders gained a reasonable 'price' for their slaves. The end result may have been the decline in the African population but that was not something Africans at the time were in a position to determine.

The beliefs and ideologies theme is reflected in Briton's ideological justification of African slavery on the basis of the Scriptures and a growing ideology based around racial difference. Such ideologies assisted Britain in the further expansion of its empire and thus in state formation.

This unit illustrates again how the themes of the module are closely linked. The next unit will build on the producers and consumers theme and consider how far slavery contributed to the Industrial Revolution in Britain.

REFERENCES

Austen, R.A. (1979) 'The trans-Saharan slave trade: a tentative census' in Gemery, H.A. and Hogendorn, J.S. (eds) *The Uncommon Market: Essays in the Economic History of the Atlantic Slave Trade*, New York, Academic Press.

Curtin, P.D. (1969) *The Atlantic Slave Trade: A Census*, Madison, University of Wisconsin Press.

Curtin, P.D. (1990) *The Rise and Fall of the Plantation Complex: Essays in Atlantic History*, Cambridge, Cambridge University Press.

Eltis, D. (1991) 'Precolonial western Africa and the Atlantic economy' in Solow (1991b).

Eltis, D. (2000) *The Rise of African Slavery in the Americas*, Cambridge, Cambridge University Press.

Eltis, D. (2001) 'The volume and structure of the transatlantic slave trade: a reassessment', *William and Mary Quarterly*, 3rd series, vol. 58, no. 1, January, pp. 17–46.

Eltis, D., Behrendt, S.D., Richardson, D. and Klein, H.S. (1999) *The Transatlantic Slave Trade: A Database on CD-ROM*, Cambridge, Cambridge University Press.

Eltis, D. and Richardson, D. (2004) 'Prices of African slaves newly arrived in the Americas, 1670–1865: new evidence on long-run trends and regional differentials' in Eltis, D., Lewis, F.D. and Sokoloff, K.L. (eds) *Slavery and the Development of the Americas*, Cambridge, Cambridge University Press.

Fogel, R.W. and Engerman, S.L. (1974) *Time on the Cross: The Economics of American Negro Slavery*, Boston, Little, Brown, 1974.

Klein, H.S. (1990) 'Economic aspects of the eighteenth-century Atlantic slave trade' in Tracy, J.D. (ed.) *The Rise of Merchant Empires: Long-Distance Trade in the Early Modern World 1350–1750*, Cambridge, Cambridge University Press.

Marshall, P.J. (ed.) (1998) *The Oxford History of the British Empire: The Eighteenth Century*, Oxford, Oxford University Press.

Price, J.M. (1991) 'Credit in the slave trade and plantation economies' in Solow (1991b).

Richardson, D. (1991) 'Prices of slaves in West and West-Central Africa: toward an annual series, 1698–1807', *Bulletin of Economic Research*, vol. 43, no. 1, pp. 21–56.

Richardson, D. (1998) 'The British Empire and the Atlantic slave trade, 1660–1807' in Marshall (1998).

Rodney, W. (1972) *How Europe Underdeveloped Africa*, London, Bogle-L'Ouverture.

Schwartz, S.B. (1987) *Sugar Plantations in the Formation of Brazilian Society: Bahia, 1550–1835*, Cambridge, Cambridge University Press.

Solow, B. (1991a) 'Slavery and colonization' in Solow (1991b).

Solow, B. (ed.) (1991b) *Slavery and the Rise of the Atlantic System*, Cambridge, Cambridge University Press.

Stein, R.L. (1979) *The French Slave Trade in the Eighteenth Century: An Old Regime Business*, Madison, University of Wisconsin Press.

Thornton, J. (1992) *Africa and Africans in the Making of the Atlantic World, 1400–1680*, Cambridge, Cambridge University Press.

Voyages (2008) *The Trans-Atlantic Slave Trade Database* [online], Atlanta, GA, Emory University, http://www.slavevoyages.org/tast/index.faces (Accessed 9 June 2011).

Ward, J.R. (1978) 'The profitability of sugar planting in the British West Indies, 1650–1834', *Economic History Review*, new series, vol. 31, no. 2, pp. 197–213.

Ward, J.R. (1998) 'The British West Indies in the age of abolition, 1748–1815' in Marshall (1998).

Watts, D. (1987) *The West Indies: Patterns of Development, Culture and Environmental Change Since 1492*, Cambridge, Cambridge University Press.

Bernard Waites and Amanda Goodrich

Learning outcomes

When you have finished this unit, you should have the knowledge, understanding and skills needed to answer and debate the following questions and historical problems.

- What was the volume and composition of British international trade and, more particularly, transatlantic colonial trade between *c.*1700 and the early nineteenth century?

- How much of this colonial trade was slave-based?

- What were the profits of this trade and how were they consumed and invested in Britain?

- Did the direct profits of slavery accruing to plantation owners, together with the indirect, commercial profits accruing to merchants who dealt in slave-grown commodities, contribute significantly to the onset of modern economic growth in late eighteenth-century, early nineteenth-century Britain?

- Was a necessary, though not sufficient, condition for industrialisation the prior creation of transatlantic markets for British manufactures, markets that derived their own purchasing power from slave-based capitalism?

- What difference did burgeoning transatlantic trade in tropical groceries make to the everyday lives of British consumers?

INTRODUCTION – TIME FOR A CUPPA?

Some people look at the tea leaves to foretell the future; let us take a cup of sweetened tea and think about the past. The national brew never passed Shakespeare's lips. Tea and sugar were great rarities well into the seventeenth century; by the 1790s, they were commonplace. According to Frederick Eden, the pioneer social investigator, they were:

> now to be met with in most cottages in southern England ... Any person who will give himself the trouble of stepping into the cottages of Middlesex and Surrey at meal times will find that, in poor families, tea is not only the usual beverage in the morning and evening, but is generally drunk in large quantities even at dinner.
>
> (Eden, 1966 [1797], vol. 3, p. 533)

What had put these erstwhile luxuries on the tables of the poor? The short answer is the globalisation of trade and slavery. Tea was shipped from China in exchange for silver, itself mined in Spanish America, and for raw cotton and opium from India. Sugar was produced by African slaves in the British West Indies. To import these commodities on such a scale that they became mundane items of household consumption, Britain had to export its own goods and services to the wider world. Had it not done so, its balance of trade would have deteriorated. To put things simply, British producers had to become more productive to consume such imported 'luxuries' as sugar, tea and tobacco. So our cup of sweetened tea connects producers and consumers in four continents.

Now, savour the leaf's sharp tang, sense the sugar rush, and think of another module theme: state formation. The intercontinental commerce that put sweetened tea on the table was not driven solely by market forces and private organisations: it intermeshed with the mercantilist state. The East India Company had a legal monopoly on all British trade east of the Cape of Good Hope, the West Indian colonial sugar producers had a monopoly on the British market. Only British owned and crewed ships could legally trade with British settlements and plantations.

We can use our cup of sweetened tea to *allude* to the connections between slavery, colonial trade, economic growth and everyday consumption in Britain. But to understand them as historians we have to work a bit harder, using aggregate data to establish the big picture. The argument that follows may appear complex, but history is – in the fashionable jargon – 'a complexity science'. If this unit has an over-riding purpose, it is to strip our sweetened tea of its aura of simplicity.

DVD exercise

Return to the notes you made when watching 'Sugar dynasty' in Unit 14 (you may also find it helpful to look at the *Media Guide* on the module website) and answer the following questions:

1   How was the wealth generated by slave labour 'consumed' (in the broadest sense of the word) by planters and plantation owners in Jamaica and Britain?
2   How did slave-produced commodities affect the everyday lives of British consumers?

Spend about 30 minutes on this exercise.

SPECIMEN ANSWER

1   In Jamaica, planters indulged in the consumption of large quantities of luxury food and drink – this excess is something that disgusts a visitor from England in the programme.

The profits from sugar created some of the largest fortunes in England, such as that of Beckford of Fonthill. Such men were often from quite humble backgrounds, their ancestors who set up the plantations being adventurers. In an attempt to distance themselves from such unsavoury ancestors and the source of their wealth in slavery, and to ally themselves instead as far as possible with the aristocracy, they often acquired vast landed estates and consumed to excess. As the programme shows, Beckford of Fonthill consumed luxury goods – ceramics, paintings, food, wine, houses – living the lifestyle of the richest nobility. They often also invested in politics. Wealth made in the empire created a new sector of rich society consisting of merchants, planters and others who had become wealthy in the colonies.

2   Sugar was exported from the West Indian plantations back to Britain, where it became a commodity enjoyed by all sectors of society. Even labourers' families could afford sugar in their tea. It was one of a number of goods being imported from the colonies, tea, of course, being another one.

In the section entitled 'Slavery, transatlantic trade and industrialisation', you will read extracts from secondary sources by Robin Blackburn and David Eltis, accessible through the A200 website, which bear directly on the question of how slave-generated wealth flowed into the British economy.

TRANSATLANTIC TRADE AND BRITISH ECONOMIC GROWTH

Unit 14 examined how the slave trade laid the foundations of the plantation economies which produced the principal commodities in early modern transatlantic trade: tobacco, coffee, rice, cocoa, indigo and, above all, sugar. Cane sugar was the single most valuable commodity import into Britain from the 1700s until the 1820s, when it was overtaken by another slave plantation crop – raw cotton. For much of this time, cane sugar was also the most valuable commodity import into France, which dominated the re-export trade in plantation produce for most of the eighteenth century. Whereas Unit 14 looked principally at Africa and the Americas, this unit has a British focus. We cannot entirely ignore French colonial trade because comparison with France is an invaluable check on arguments about the connections between New World slavery and British economic growth. If slave-based commercial capitalism was a springboard for industrial capitalism in Britain, then it should have played a similar role in France.

The purpose of this section is to establish the value, geography and composition of British foreign trade between *c*.1690 and 1815 and then to ask how important foreign trade was in the onset of modern economic growth.[1]

We are better informed about foreign trade than most aspects of the early modern British economy because of a relative abundance of quantitative data, derived from customs and excise returns. Taxes on imports have always been a convenient source of state revenue: they are inexpensive to raise and alienate fewer interest groups than land or income taxes because they tend to fall on luxuries, such as sugar. During the French wars (1793–1815) the escalating sugar duties were the most important single source of government revenue, accounting for one-eighth of all taxation in Britain.

Useful though foreign trade data are for economic historians, their interpretation is problematic, for several reasons. The taxation of trade is always an incentive to smuggling, and we can only guess at the dimensions of illegal trade. Sugar is bulky and requires sophisticated handling and storage facilities, so it is unlikely that substantial quantities were smuggled into Britain (but tobacco and tea were easily and profitably smuggled). In certain years, illegal imports probably accounted for a third of consumption. Imports and exports were recorded at 'official values', which diverged from market values as prices rose in the late eighteenth and early nineteenth centuries. The technical difficulties of converting 'official' to market values need not concern us, since scholars have concluded that the 'official' series are a fairly reliable indicator of changes in *volumes*. There is, however, a more intractable problem bedevilling the data on the re-export of 'colonial' produce, which formed a very substantial part of total foreign trade by 1800. When colonial commodities were re-exported, merchants were allowed three years to 'draw back' the duties paid when the goods entered Britain. This led both to delays in invoicing re-exports and their over-valuation, with the result that the quantities re-exported sometimes appeared to exceed imports.

| EXERCISE | Tables 15.1–15.3 show the regional distribution of British domestic (i.e. home produced) exports and re-exports, and the regional sources of British imports during the eighteenth century. In case there is any confusion, trade between Scotland and England was internal trade and does not figure in these statistics, but trade between mainland Britain and the 'British Islands' (Ireland, the Channel Islands) was counted as foreign trade. The reference to 'Great Britain' in the tables includes Scotland. Look carefully at the data and summarise the main trends. Bear in mind the outbreak of the American War of Independence (1775–83) and of the French revolutionary wars. |

Spend about 30 minutes on this exercise.

---

[1] Until 1707, Scottish trade was under a separate jurisdiction and even after the union Scottish trade statistics were collected separately. The data on the eighteenth century in a standard reference work (Mitchell and Deane, 1962) cover England and Wales up to 1772 (or 1791 in the case of specific items), Great Britain thereafter. Scotland accounted for about 9 per cent of British foreign trade in 1780. Trade with Ireland, a commercial colony of Britain, is separately itemised up to 1791. The British and Irish customs were not amalgamated until the 1820s.

Table 15.1 The destination of British domestic exports (£k, official values)

	Europe	British Islands (Ireland etc.)	Americas (inc. the West Indies)	Asia	Africa
1700–01 (England and Wales)	3,660 (82%)	144 (3%)	461 (10%)	114 (3%)	81 (2%)
1772–73 (England and Wales)	3,883 (40%)	912 (9%)	3,628 (37%)	824 (8%)	492 (5%)
1797–98 (Great Britain)	3,858 (21%)	1,641 (9%)	10,312 (56%)	1,640 (9%)	650 (4%)

(Source: Mitchell and Deane, 1962)

Table 15.2 The destination of British re-exports (£k, official values)

	Europe	British Islands (Ireland etc.)	Americas (inc. the West Indies)	Asia	Africa
1700–01 (England and Wales)	1,652 (77%)	159 (7%)	237 (11%)	11 (1%)	64 (3%)
1772–73 (England and Wales)	3,655 (63%)	1,102 (19%)	691 (12%)	69 (1%)	285 (5%)
1797–98 (Great Britain)	9,150 (78%)	1,286 (11%)	853 (7%)	75 (1%)	437 (4%)

(Source: Mitchell and Deane, 1962)

Table 15.3 The source of British imports (£k, official values)

	Europe	British Islands (Ireland etc.)	Americas (inc. the West Indies)	Asia	Africa
1700–01 (England and Wales)	3,578 (61%)	285 (4%)	1,157 (20%)	775 (13%)	34 (1%)
1772–73 (England and Wales)	4,301 (35%)	1,303 (10%)	4,522 (36%)	2,203 (18%)	80 (1%)
1797–98 (Great Britain)	7,003 (29%)	3,127 (13%)	7,678 (32%)	5,785 (24%)	62 (1%)

(Source: Mitchell and Deane, 1962)

SPECIMEN ANSWER

With respect to exports, the most striking trends are the growth of markets in the Caribbean and continental America for British domestic exports and the stagnation of European markets. At the beginning of the eighteenth century, Europe absorbed four-fifths of domestic exports; at the end, one-fifth. Over the course of the eighteenth century, Ireland took a greater share of domestic exports, and provided a greater share of imports, and the Asian share of British imports also rose. Although, as Table 15.2 shows, British re-exports to Europe remained buoyant, Tables 15.1 and 15.3

show that both British domestic exports and imports declined. This shows the partial decoupling of the British economy from Europe and its increasing dependence on other countries as markets for British domestic exports and imports.

DISCUSSION

These tables reveal the growing significance of transatlantic markets for British producers and shippers, and the British economy more broadly. Trade with the thirteen colonies collapsed during the American War of Independence, but this was clearly a temporary reversal since the 'Americanisation' of the domestic export trades accelerated with the restoration of peace. By 1800, nearly three-fifths of domestic exports went to the Americas. Independence freed Americans from the Navigation Laws and they now could import tea, coffee and sugar from wherever they chose, which explains the relative decline of re-exports going to the Americas (Table 15.2). A point worth adding is that the 'Americanisation' of domestic exporting was all the more remarkable when we consider that Europe's population was about 200 million in 1800, while the combined population of the Americas was perhaps 15 million.[2]

Now let us consider the changing commodity structure of imports, domestic exports and re-exports as revealed by Table 15.4 (by commodity structure we mean the balance between manufactures, raw materials and foodstuffs). This provides three snapshots of the main goods shipped into and out of England and Wales in 1700 and 1760 and into and out of Britain in 1800. The table looks complicated and forbidding. So, rather than set a formal exercise, we have chosen to talk you through what we can deduce about the commodity structure of English/British trade at each snapshot and the major changes that occurred between them. Bear in mind that we are dealing with official values, not physical quantities: the two-and-a-half-fold increase in sugar import values between 1700 and 1760 does not mean that physical imports increased two and a half times. In fact, sugar was somewhat cheaper in 1760 and the quantity imported had risen more than three-fold.

The 1700 snapshot

In 1700, the commodity structure of English foreign trade reflected the country's commercial integration with Europe. Woollen goods accounted for nearly three-quarters of domestic exports by value. You should note that, apart from a small quantity of coal, nearly all domestic exports were manufactures or semi-manufactures of some description, a sign that England had a comparative advantage in both lush pastures (for breeding sheep for wool) and handicraft skills. England was self-sufficient in corn (corn here refers to all edible cereal grains), but imported wine and raw materials for her textile trades and ship-building. The balance of trade was virtually neutral: imports were officially valued at £5.84 million, domestic exports at £3.73 million and re-exports at £2.08 million. This snapshot would have been broadly familiar to

[2] The population of the USA in 1800 was 5.3 million; the population of Latin America and the Caribbean may have been 10 million, though this is probably an overestimate.

Table 15.4 The commodity structure of British trade in 1700, 1760 and 1800

	Principal imports, value (£)				Principal domestic exports, value (£)				Re-exports, value (£)		
	1700	1760	1800		1700	1760	1800		1700	1760	1800
Corn	–	–	2,673	Coal	68	136	510				
Coffee	36	257	3,988	Iron and steel	90	539	1,605	Coffee	2		
Sugar	668	1,799	4,301	Non-ferrous metals and manufactures	263	494	1,414	Sugar	49	156	11,068
Tea	14	969	1,510	Cotton yarn and manufactures	24	167	5,851	Tea	2	256[†]	
Wine	647	371	732	Woollen yarn and manufactures	2,697	5,453	6,918				
Timber	119	147	582	Linen yarn and manufactures	7	557	808				
Raw wool	220	91	500	Silk yarn and manufactures	69	348	297	Piece-goods	746[†]	1,353[†]	2,664
Silk	377	626	739								
Raw cotton	–	–	1,430					Tobacco	421[†]		624
Tobacco	315	491	357								
Iron	182	289	375								
Flax	110	128	795								
Hemp	71	58	507								
Linen yarn	46	232	506								
Other	3,035			Other	513	3,287		Other			
Total imports	5,840 (E&W)	9,833 (E&W)	30,571 (GB)	Total domestic exports	3,731 (E&W)	10,981 (E&W)	24,304 (GB)	Total re-exports	2,081 (E&W)	3,714 (E&W)	18,848 (GB)

E&W = England and Wales, GB = Great Britain
* = value of coffee, sugar and tea re-exports combined
(Sources: Schumpeter, 1960, and Mitchell and Deane, 1962; except for † = data from Davis, 1962)

the early Tudors, but there was one novel element: the already substantial share of 'colonial' groceries (sugar, tobacco, coffee and tea) in the import schedule – together they accounted for over 17 per cent of imports. Sugar had been a rare luxury in Tudor times; in 1700, the value of sugar imports exceeded that of wine.

The 1760 snapshot

Several trends are evident. First, foreign trade values had grown very markedly. As the bottom row of the table shows, total imports were now officially valued at £9.833 million (a 68 per cent increase on 1700), but the value of total domestic exports had risen much more rapidly. The total stood at £10.981 million, nearly a three-fold increase on 1700. The balance of trade was highly favourable: combined exports and re-exports exceeded imports by £4.862 million. Second, woollens were still the most important item in the export schedule, their domestic export value nearly doubling from 1700. However, their share of the total export value had fallen from 72 per cent to 49 per cent. Exports of linen, silk and cotton goods, and iron and steel had all increased at a much faster rate. Third, a large proportion of imports now arrived by oceanic rather than short-haul trade, and reflected British imperial and naval power. Imports of tea from China, the sole source at this time, had been negligible in 1700; by 1760, they had risen phenomenally. Imports of wine were much reduced. Sugar, tea, coffee and tobacco accounted for 36 per cent of all imports; if we were to include exotic fruits, rice, ginger, etc., then tropical or semi-tropical groceries made up two-fifths of imports. Except for tea, these were slave-grown crops.

The 1800 snapshot

This reveals an extraordinary growth of re-exports. They had increased five-fold since 1760, while imports had roughly tripled in value and domestic exports had roughly doubled. Re-exports handsomely corrected the unfavourable balance of domestic trade. You should note, too, that corn appears in the import schedule, indicating that Britain was no longer self-sufficient in food grains. Substantial quantities of raw cotton were also imported for the first time. These raw cotton imports lay behind the thirty-five-fold increase in cotton exports since 1760, and testify to the emergence of a dynamic, export-oriented industry in Lancashire. There is an anomaly in the data which you may have spotted: tobacco re-exports were, seemingly, nearly twice the value of tobacco imports: how are we to explain that? Had all pipe-smokers and snuff-takers suddenly quit the weed? Surely not; smuggling, delayed re-exporting and the over-valuation of re-exports may all have been involved.

Discussion

As we have seen (Tables 15.1–15.3), transatlantic and Asian markets became more significant than Europe for British trade during the eighteenth century except for re-exports, which continued to go primarily to Europe. As Table 15.4 shows, re-exports were all goods imported from the Americas and Asia.

The 1800 data raise interesting questions about popular consumption that are germane to a later section. Coffee, sugar, tea and tobacco accounted for a third of all imports, but 62 per cent of re-exports. There is no particular virtue in selling goods to foreigners that could have been sold at home and it is difficult to believe that the home market was saturated. Living standards, we might conclude, were not rising fast enough to absorb the quantities available at the prevailing prices, which were inflated by high wartime duties, with Britain at war with France. To which we must add there is a particular problem gauging the true scale of coffee imports and re-exports because the data are distorted by official over-valuation. Coffee imports *appear* to have risen ten-fold in the 1790s, but not because the British were seized by a craze for caffeine. Nearly all coffee was re-exported to European markets, which before 1791 had been supplied by St Domingue and other French islands.

The export data for cotton manufactures testify to the industry's role as the leading sector in early industrialisation, but beware of reading more change into the data than had actually occurred. Retained imports of raw sugar were worth considerably more than raw cotton imports in 1800, and sugar refining was a substantial 'industry', to use the word in its broadest sense. Imported sugar was not fit for the table, because planters in British colonies were prohibited from processing beyond the so-called muscovado stage.[3] All had to be refined before it could be distributed and sold, so substantial value was added in Britain. The industry was a useful foreign earner, since 'refined sugar' was classed with *domestic* exports, and accounted for 4.5 per cent of the total in 1800. Cotton yarn was mostly machine spun using water power, but cotton weaving was no more industrialised than sugar refining; in neither had machines and inanimate power been substituted for human effort and skill on any great scale.

From the extraordinary total of re-exports in 1800, one could argue that the buoyancy of Britain's foreign trade sector depended as much on military might and shipping services as on the inherent strength of manufacturing. True, the schedule of domestic exports in 1800 was dominated by manufactures, as it had been in 1700, but *virtually all the increment was sold in relatively easy transatlantic markets*. Prior to the American war, the colonists had no choice but to depend on British suppliers for imports of manufactures, since the Trade and Navigation Acts effectively excluded all foreign goods. During the war, when Britain was confronted by the 'armed neutrality' of the major European powers, as well as the rebellious colonists and their French allies, exports slumped by about a third. With the resumption of peace, the Americans could import from whom they chose, and preferred British manufactures over all others. Does this demonstrate their quality and competitive price? Perhaps, but

---

[3] What the eighteenth century called 'muscovado sugar' was perhaps muckier stuff than the packet of brown sugar labelled 'muscovado' today.

don't forget American import prices had to cover transport and insurance, sectors in which the British were very efficient. In 1806, when the Napoleonic system of economic boycott had closed many European markets for British goods, US customers bought about 35 per cent of British domestic exports and other American markets purchased a further 30 per cent. The closure of Europe to British goods had been partly compensated for by commercial access to the Spanish and Portuguese empires.

Export data are not very meaningful unless we can relate them to the totality of economic activity (gross national product – GNP) and the total output of manufacturing (gross industrial product – GIP) – see Table 15.5.

Table 15.5   Domestic exports as a proportion of gross national product (GNP) and industrial output + increase in exports as a proportion of increase in GNP

	(a) Domestic exports as a proportion of GNP	(b) Domestic exports as a proportion of industrial output	(c) Increase in exports as a proportion of increase in GNP
1700	8.4%	24%	
1760	14.6%	35%	1700–60: 30.4%
1780	9.4%	22%	1760–80: 5.1%
1801	15.7%	34%	1780–1801: 21%

(Source: Crafts, 1985, p. 131)

Table 15.5 provides estimates of the ratio of exports to GNP and industrial output. We are dealing with an economy in the pre-statistical age so the speculative character of the data must be emphasised. Caveats aside, what do they tell us? Let's begin with columns (a) and (b). These show that the proportion of total domestic output exported in 1700 was 8–9 per cent of GNP, which was already quite high by historical standards. It would seem that around a quarter of manufactured output was sold abroad and so one in four non-agricultural workers already depended for their livelihood on foreign markets. The proportion increased significantly up to 1760, when the ratio of domestic exports to GNP of 14–15 per cent and just over a third of industrial output was being exported. This ratio was exceptionally high for a medium-sized pre-industrial economy. If you look at column (c), you will see that rising exports between 1700 and 1760 accounted for 30 per cent of the increase in GNP. You will observe there was a severe check to exports' contribution to the growth of total output around 1780, caused principally by the American war. You should note that, though domestic exports recovered in the 1780s and 1790s, when the pace of industrialisation quickened, their contribution to the growth of total output was less than it had been in earlier decades.

The information you have acquired so far in studying this unit should enable you to answer the first question in the learning outcomes at the beginning of the unit: 'What was the volume and composition of British international trade, and more particularly, transatlantic colonial trade between *c*.1700 and the early nineteenth century?'

EXERCISE

Now consider this additional question: what have you learned about the significance of New World slavery for British commerce?

Spend a few minutes on this exercise.

SPECIMEN ANSWER

As Tables 15.3 and 15.4 show, imports from the Americas (including the West Indies) of sugar, coffee, tobacco and cotton (all produced by slave labour) grew greatly during the eighteenth century, and the first three of these commodities also contributed to a buoyant re-export market to Europe. One-third of the commodity imports into late eighteenth-century Britain were produced by slaves and nearly three-fifths of domestic exports were going to transatlantic markets where slaves were an important, if not the principal, source of labour. Thus slaves were important producers of Britain's imports and re-exports.

EXPORTS AND THE INDUSTRIAL REVOLUTION

The Industrial Revolution

The Industrial Revolution in Britain has a long and complex historiography. In the late nineteenth century, historians such as A. Toynbee (1884), in his *Lectures on the Industrial Revolution in England*, identified it in terms of an industrial and economic 'take-off', which began in the second half of the eighteenth century. Central to this process was, first, technological innovation: the development of machinery, mechanised factories and steam power, resulting in both industrial and social transformation. Second, structural change in the labour force reflected fewer labourers working in agriculture and increasing numbers working in manufacturing and services. This interpretation, among others, persisted into the 1960s among some historians such as W.W. Rostow and E.P. Thompson. Thereafter, the historiography has moved away from the idea of a 'take-off', and historians such as N.F.R. Crafts, J.G. Williamson, D. Cannadine, M. Berg and P. Hudson have identified a longer, slower and more uneven process that stretched back to the end of the seventeenth or early eighteenth century and extended long into the nineteenth (e.g. Crafts, 1987; Williamson, 1987; Cannadine, 1987; Berg and Hudson, 1992[4]).

In brief, it is now clear that technological innovation did not result in widespread mechanised, factory-based manufacture in the latter part of the eighteenth century. Despite the invention of the steam engine in the eighteenth century, it did not have significant impact in industry until at

---

[4] You came across this article by Berg and Hudson ('Rehabilitating the Industrial Revolution', *Economic History Review*, vol. 45, no. 1, pp. 24–50, from JSTOR) in Unit 13. If you did not read it all then and would like to learn more about this topic, you may like to read the whole article now.

least 1850. While the cotton mills in the north-west did introduce mechanised factory systems for cotton spinning and the iron industry experienced considerable technical innovation in the eighteenth century, most traditional manufactures, such as glass making, brewing, leather working and small metal trades, remained unmechanised in small workshops until well into the nineteenth century, relying on artisanal or handicraft skills. There was growth in manufacturing and technological development, but both of these occurred for the most part in unmechanised manufacturing industries. Growth in manufacture and trade were assisted by new commercial systems such as marketing, retailing and wholesaling, and increased use of credit, insurance and banking. Communication and distribution systems improved dramatically in the eighteenth century and as a result regional specialisations developed, such as small metal-working sectors in Birmingham and Sheffield, pottery in Staffordshire, and specialist handicrafts and fashion items in London. In terms of the structure of the workforce, the shift away from agricultural work and to urban occupations became notable early in the eighteenth century – although, of those working in manufacturing, the majority worked in smaller workshops, and in the putting-out system. It was in the nineteenth century that increasing numbers worked as labourers in mechanised factories. As explained in Unit 13, there is now something of a consensus over the issue of industrialisation in the eighteenth century

You should now know more about the value, geography and commodity structure of foreign trade, but what was its significance for the onset of the Industrial Revolution? The standard account of the Industrial Revolution in terms of trade portrays it as an *endogenous* process: that is to say, internally driven by population growth, improved productivity in agriculture and services, and rising incomes. Exports were, accordingly, a secondary factor. Advocates of the standard account do not dispute that an increasing proportion of manufacturing output was exported, but it was – they argue – the strength of the domestic economy that enabled British manufacturers to sell in export markets, not export markets that strengthened the domestic economy. In a study of the long-run growth of the economy, Phyllis Deane and W. A. Cole pointed out that exports grew most rapidly when Britain was having to sell more abroad to fund its imports of tropical groceries and raw materials. When this was not the case, the rate of export growth declined. For Deane and Cole, the underlying dynamic in the expansion of international trade (imports and exports combined) was the *demand for imports* in Britain, a society where incomes were rising and consumer preferences were changing. They concluded 'if we want to understand the growing import demand [in eighteenth-century Britain] we must look for the factors which promoted economic expansion at home' (Deane and Cole, 1967, p. 89).

Why should we question this standard account? The reason is that the comparative study of industrialisation has revealed that structural change began at a very early stage in Britain. By about 1750, manufacturing, building, commerce and the professions already accounted for about 45 per cent of labour force allocation (Crafts, 1985, p. 13). Britain was unusual in undergoing such 'precocious' structural change; apart from the Netherlands, no other economy experienced such a pronounced shift of labour from agriculture to manufacturing at such an early stage. Moreover, the evidence suggests that in real terms wages did not rise significantly until well into the nineteenth century. Indeed, Britain was unique in the history of industrialising economies in having such a large proportion of manufactures in its domestic export schedule when the average income level was still very low. Those arguing that the Industrial Revolution was export led stress the role of foreign markets in raising the level of aggregate demand for manufacturing capital, labour and commercial services, and so boosting the growth of secondary and tertiary employment and capital investment in Britain.[5] For an economy the size of Britain's, international trade was – so they maintain – a necessary condition for an extended market, a more complex division of labour and industrial specialisation. Ralph Davis was one of the first historians to make the connection between the dynamism of colonial exporting and the advance of manufacturing:

> The process of industrialisation in England from the second quarter of the eighteenth century was to an important extent a response to colonial demands for nails, axes, firearms, buckets, coaches, clocks, saddles, handkerchiefs, buttons, cordage, and a thousand other things ... In the iron and brass industries and all the metal-working crafts dependent on them, colonial demands made an important supplement to the growing home market, and must have played a considerable part in encouraging the new methods of organisation, the new forms of division of labour and improved techniques, through which the metal industries were to make a major contribution to industrial revolution in England.
>
> (Davis, 1962, p. 290)

This section has gone some way towards answering the fifth question in the learning outcomes at the beginning of this unit: structural change in the labour force – the movement of workers out of agriculture and into manufacturing and services – was to a significant extent induced by rising transatlantic demand for British manufactures.

SLAVERY, TRANSATLANTIC TRADE AND INDUSTRIALISATION

So what has this got to do with slavery and slave-based production? For a short answer, see the intriguingly entitled *Africans and the Industrial Revolution in England*, by Joseph Inikori, a Nigerian scholar who has long

---

[5] If you are unfamiliar with the terms, primary employment refers to work in agriculture, fishing and forestry; secondary, to manufacturing, processing, building and construction, and – usually – mining; tertiary, to work providing services (shopkeeping, schoolteaching, etc).

been working on Atlantic history in the USA. Inikori's argument focuses on the vital contribution of Atlantic commerce to the expansion of early modern international trade and the overwhelming importance of African slaves as producers of the commodities exported from the Americas. Free wage labour was scarce and expensive in continental America because the abundance of fertile land meant white indentured workers could easily become independent farmers after completing their labour contract. Large-scale commodity production was made possible only by importing African slaves, whose cheap labour enabled a growing number of European consumers to enjoy American commodity exports. The income from export sales in turn created American markets for British cloth, hardware, pottery and other manufactures, so raising the level of demand in the secondary and tertiary sectors of the British economy. The dynamic impact of Atlantic commerce on the British economy did not, Inikori argues, stem solely from Anglophone America. British-manufactured exports to Portugal and Spain were largely paid for by income generated in Iberian America, where African slaves produced sugar, coffee and cocoa, and were the mainstay of gold mining in Columbia and Minas Gerais.[6] Moreover, looking at the manufacturing sector of the economy as whole tends to disguise the crucial contribution of transatlantic sales to the expansion of production. If, as Inikori urges, we focus on the developing industrial *regions* (Lancashire, the West Riding of Yorkshire, the west Midlands) we find their dependence on New World export markets was much greater than that of the long-established manufacturing centres of East Anglia and the south-west. Inikori concludes:

> The centrality of Atlantic commerce to the development process in England is the real measure of the contribution of Africans to the British Industrial Revolution. Apart from the forced labour of American Indians employed in the production of silver in Spanish America, enslaved Africans and their descendants were the only specialised producers of commodities in the Americas for Atlantic commerce.
>
> (Inikori, 2002, p. 481)

Inikori's argument is not entirely novel: when reviewing the role of exports in the growth of the British economy up to the 1770s, Patrick O'Brien and Stan Engerman underlined 'the significance of sea power, imperial connections, slavery, and mercantilist regulation for the sale of British manufactures overseas' (O'Brien and Engerman, 1991, p. 186). Where Inikori departs from other scholars is in asserting that without the export markets created by slavery and colonial commerce, industrial growth would have faltered and the British economy would have reached a plateau. Insufficient demand would have led manufacturing to stagnate, so there would have been less incentive to invest in

---

[6] Minas Gerais is a highland region about 480 kilometres (300 miles) north of Rio de Janeiro where gold was discovered in 1695; about 30,000 black slaves were mining gold around 1715.

technological innovation; capital would instead have flowed into commerce and financial services.

A critique of Inikori's thesis

Inikori has made an arresting case for making modern economic growth dependent on New World slavery. Is it intellectually persuasive? One criticism might be that it overstates the role of slavery in New World markets, which need disaggregating. These markets included Caribbean islands, where slaves were the great majority of the population, but also Pennsylvania and New England, which instituted gradual emancipation from 1780 onward and where political and social freedom were more entrenched than in Britain. The free, white population was increasing rapidly, and its purchasing power was several times greater than that of the slaves and slave owners: exports to the USA substantially exceeded exports to the British Caribbean from 1785 through to 1810. So can we assume that slavery's role in the growth of Atlantic trade was diminishing just as the tempo of British industrial growth was quickening? That would be a too hasty conclusion. The USA (particularly the northern states) ran a considerable deficit in Anglo-American trade. Transport costs restricted the British market for American produce to Virginia tobacco, Carolina rice and indigo, and, from the late 1790s, raw cotton, which were all slave-grown. So how did Pennsylvanians and New Englanders settle their accounts with their British suppliers? They could have shipped bullion across the Atlantic, but they mostly paid with credit notes, using earnings made by exporting food, rum and other supplies to the southern states, the Caribbean and Africa. In other words, slavery had a crucial role in the *multilateral* settlement of transatlantic trading accounts around 1800.

Had the United States remained within the territorial boundaries of the thirteen colonies, then we could envisage a steadily diminishing role for slavery in Atlantic trade, partly because the country was becoming more self-sufficient as the northern states developed their own manufactures. But the purchase of Louisiana in 1803[7] doubled the size of the nation and hugely expanded the area in which slaves would, in future decades, be the principal producers of export commodities.

Inikori's thesis can perhaps be more justly criticised, for understating the complexity and resilience of the British economy and overstating its dependence on Atlantic markets. They absorbed between one-sixth and one-fifth of British manufactured output in the last quarter of the eighteenth century: a sizeable proportion, to be sure, but insufficiently large to have the make-or-break developmental and demographic effects imputed to it. During the two conflicts with North America (1775–83, 1812–14) the British home market proved ample enough to prevent industrial collapse. But a more

---

[7] 'Louisiana' refers to all the French territories on the North American mainland, which Napoleon sold to the USA in 1803.

damaging criticism is that the thesis conflates those analytically distinct components of industrialisation that were mentioned above: structural change and technical innovation.

Slavery was behind the growth of Atlantic trade and, because it extended the market, was a factor in 'precocious' structural change in Britain, but did it stimulate technological innovation? The links between slavery and British industrialisation *in this sense* were surely tenuous to the point of irrelevance. Its dynamics – common to much of Europe – were an exceptional technical creativity in harnessing natural forces for economically productive purposes and a competence in machine building unmatched by any other culture. There were, of course, manifest connections between cotton – the prototype machine industry – and slavery, but the causal relationship mostly worked from Britain *outwards*, with rising demand for raw cotton resulting in the extension of the slave plantation system. The mechanisation of cotton spinning is a classic instance of the shortage of an industrial input stimulating technical progress, for innovation began around 1770 in response to bottlenecks in the supply of yarn when the fledgling industry still obtained much of its raw material through the Levant. The productivity gains of mechanised spinning lowered the price of yarn dramatically, and led to increased demand both for cotton textiles and cotton fibre. Raw cotton imports rose eight-fold between 1780 and 1800, with Caribbean and Brazilian slave plantations meeting nearly all the rising demand. Obviously, there was a feedback from the New World as abundant supplies of cheap fibre became an incentive to further investment in cotton manufacturing in Britain. But mechanical innovation and the displacement of manual skills affected only the spinning and preparatory processes until the 1820s and 1830s, when power looms were introduced on a considerable scale. The cotton textiles that conquered overseas markets in the 1800s were woven by domestic handicraft workers using traditional techniques. By providing handloom weavers with cheap yarn, slavery enabled them to compete with the power loom for at least twenty years after the first viable model was patented.

You should now understand the case for regarding slave-based transatlantic markets as a necessary, though not sufficient, condition for British industrialisation. You may have been entirely persuaded of its merits, but it perhaps needs modifying. With respect to structural change in the labour force, the case is fairly robust; with respect to technological innovation – surely an essential aspect of industrialisation – it is weaker.

THE PROFITS OF SLAVERY AND THE EMERGENCE OF INDUSTRIAL CAPITALISM

Up to this point, we have focused on slavery and the extension of the market. Now, we turn to slavery and capital accumulation. What is meant by 'capital accumulation'? Well, we all know businesses must re-invest some of their profits to expand. The re-invested profits go into capital goods (let us say machines) which raise productivity and result in greater output. That, in a nutshell, is capital accumulation. What is true of businesses is equally true of national economies. To expand, they must raise their level of investment (accumulate capital) so that productivity rises and total national output grows. How poor agrarian economies, in which many lived close to subsistence, began the cycle of capital accumulation is one of the great conundrums of world economic history: they tended to become trapped at a low income level as population pressure forced people onto marginal land with a declining rate of return. Eighteenth-century Britain clearly broke out of this trap and entered a qualitatively new phase of economic growth. Were the exceptional profits of slavery a significant contributory factor in that process? Several scholars have argued they were, most notably Eric Williams, a Trinidadian Marxist who later became his country's first prime minister. His *Capitalism and Slavery* (first published in 1944) remains an influential discussion of the historical relation between Caribbean slavery and the development of the British economy (Williams, 1961 [1944]). Its central contentions were that the slave trade and colonial slavery first paved the way for industrial capitalism by creating a stream of investment funds, and were ultimately abolished because they had ceased to be economically profitable.

Parts of the 'Williams thesis' are no longer tenable in the light of subsequent research into both the profitability of the slave plantation complex and the development of the British economy. He greatly exaggerated the contribution of slave trading itself to capital accumulation in Britain: its profit level was under 10 per cent, and total investment derived from the slave trade was only £14,000 a year (or a derisory 0.11 per cent of total investment) (Anstey, 1975, Table 1, pp. 47, 51). As you will see in the next unit, the abolition of the trade was not economically determined, nor was the slave plantation complex in inexorable economic decline in the early nineteenth century. Furthermore, Williams overestimated the investment required for Britain's industrialisation because he, along with most economic historians of his generation, believed it swiftly transformed production techniques and business organisation. In fact, as we have seen, much manufacturing remained small-scale well into the nineteenth century. The investment requirements of the economy were, therefore, low: only 8 per cent of national income was devoted to investment in 1800, and 10.5 per cent in 1840. Countries industrialising later allocated much larger proportions of national income to investment. Williams imagined a surge of industrial investment, swollen by West Indian profits; in reality, this was not the case.

So what remains of value in the 'Williams thesis'? Some historians would say 'very little indeed'; others, that he correctly identified slavery's role in the emergence of modern, industrial capitalism. To explore those conflicting arguments you need to access the extracts from Blackburn and Eltis on the A200 website.

EXERCISE

Turn to the extract from the secondary source by Robin Blackburn, 'Primitive accumulation and British industrialization', on the A200 website. Blackburn's point of departure is Marx's concept of 'primitive accumulation' which, in volume 1 of *Capital*, helps explain the transformation of the feudal mode of production into the capitalist mode. In a capitalist economy, Marx argued, entrepreneurs profit by exploiting free wage labour; workers are paid less than the value they add in producing commodities. Entrepreneurs re-invest their profits in new or extended enterprises, thus accumulating capital. But the capitalist mode of production could not have originated this way, for there was no large class of free wage earners to exploit. There must have been some other way to kick start the cycle of investment, commodity production, profit and re-investment. Marx believed that the violent expansion of early modern Europe into the wider world provided such a stimulus: naked conquest and coercion led to the 'primitive accumulation' of resources in Europe; a process systematised in late seventeenth-century England when the state assumed new economic functions (such as managing the national debt and protecting domestic manufactures) while throwing its military power behind the colonial system (Marx, 1976 [1867], pp. 915–18). For Blackburn, 'the slave economies count as a form of "primitive" accumulation because their productive organization was based on non-economic coercion; the direct producers were obliged by brute force to produce a surplus and a marketable commodity' (Blackburn, 1997, p. 2).

Bearing this in mind, read what Blackburn has to say and answer these questions:

1   Does he defend the idea that industrialisation required a surge of investment? If not, why is investment a relevant issue? To what other types of investment does he draw our attention?

2   Does Blackburn claim that the profits of sugar production and distribution would themselves have greatly augmented the stream of investment funds? If not, what other profits does he regard as a source of 'primitive accumulation'?

3   Does he demonstrate that the direct and indirect profits of the 'triangular trade' supplied a substantial proportion of Britain's capital requirements?

4   What is the empirical evidence for industrial capitalism developing in close, causal connection with the 'triangular trade'?

Spend about 2 hours on this exercise.

SPECIMEN ANSWER

1   No; but investment remains a relevant issue because a commercial society trading much of its output abroad had to invest heavily in its transport infrastructure (canals, roads, harbours, docks) and urban improvements. Moreover, merchants and other entrepreneurs always needed working capital or commercial credit, which called for financial investment.

2   No; sugar profits could not in themselves have greatly augmented the stream of investment funds – though a substantial 'industry', sugar production and distribution were a small part of total production. However, substantial profits were realised by industries such as woollens, iron and, later, cotton textiles in New World and African markets, which would have been a fraction of their actual size without slavery.

3   No, he doesn't. He demonstrates that, on a conservative estimate, these profits *could have* supplied between a fifth and a third of Britain's capital requirements. However, just because they could have been used for productive investment does not mean they were. Perhaps West Indian fortunes commonly found their way into country seats or extravaganzas such as Fonthill, which added little to the economy's productive capacity. He does argue that the profits of slavery and empire helped to make possible the major investment in infrastructure, agriculture and industrial development, by increasing the resources available to public authorities. But the systems were inefficient by today's standards and investment was not always made appropriately.

4   Empirical evidence has been found in the symbiosis between Liverpool merchants in the triangular trade and manufacturers in the developing Lancashire textile industry. The merchants depended on local manufacturers (often unmechanised) for the supply of their most important trade goods, and so advanced credit. Manufacturers depended on export markets for long runs and economies of scale. Very little of the cotton industry's investment resources came from outside Lancashire; to a remarkable degree, it evolved within the Atlantic-facing mercantile complex based on Liverpool and Manchester.

EXERCISE

Now turn to the extract from the secondary source by David Eltis, 'Europe and the Atlantic slave systems', on the A200 website. Eltis is possibly the sharpest critic of the 'Williams thesis', although he does not actually engage directly with Williams's text in the extract. The extract from his work is shorter than that from Blackburn; read it and answer these questions:

1   How, according to Eltis, should we think about the sugar islands in relation to the British economy?

2   What does he say about the economic significance of the Atlantic slave trade for Britain?

3   What is his riposte to the argument that the triangular trade's direct and indirect profits could have generated a considerable proportion of investment funds?

4   There is a catch in arguing that, since the slave plantation complex generated such fabulous profits, they must have swelled the stream of investment funds; what is that catch?

5   Eltis insists we look at the relationship between the plantation complex and economic growth in a comparative perspective; how does this advance the argument?

Spend about 45 minutes on this exercise.

SPECIMEN ANSWER

1   To gauge the real significance of the sugar islands for the British economy, we should think of them as specialised parts of the domestic economy that happened to be located thousands of miles of way. Their trade with the metropolis was more like trade between town and country than international trade; it is an accident of fiscal policy that we know so much about it. Viewed in

this light, the sugar islands appear as small additions to a rapidly growing whole. The combined population of Barbados and Jamaica was about 300,000 in 1775, much smaller than that of Ulster, where the booming linen industry was located.

2   The slave trade formed a tiny share of Britain's Atlantic trade and accounted for few of her ships; its contribution to economic growth was 'trivial'.

3   So could many other industries and their related trades. Although sugar was a big business around 1800, output and value added were several times greater in other industries, such as iron and woollens, which had stronger linkages to the rest of the economy. Their profits were absolutely, if not relatively, greater and rather more likely to flow into productive investment.

4   Those insisting on the stupendous profits made producing sugar must explain the incentive to shift savings to other sectors. If the rate of return was so attractive, why weren't sugar profits simply ploughed back into extending the sugar frontier?

5   The obsessive pursuit of causal links between New World slavery and British industrialisation looks bizarre in a *comparative* perspective. If any European economy should have been propelled into modern economic growth by the profits of slavery it was Portugal's. Relative to its population – one-third the size of England's in the eighteenth century – Portugal's slave plantation sector was the largest of all the European powers. Portuguese and Brazilian capitalists must have invested a much larger proportion of national income in slaving and slave-based production than their British counterparts. Yet Portugal was steadily marginalised in the Atlantic 'world': it lacked internal transport systems, could not feed its own population, depended increasingly on imported manufactures, and was probably the poorest country in western Europe when the slave trade was finally suppressed. The French counter-example is equally pertinent. For much of the eighteenth century more slaves laboured in the French Caribbean, producing substantially more plantation produce, than in British America. In 1791, the slave population of the French empire was 50 per cent greater than that of the British and they produced considerably more plantation produce. France was a great manufacturing and commercial nation: the value of her transatlantic colonial trade rose six-fold between 1730 and 1776, a faster rate of increase than Britain's. By 1750, colonial commodities – sugar, coffee, indigo – represented more than half of French sales to the Dutch. Yet, though economic historians have traced the origins of modern French economic growth to the final decades of the *ancien régime*, none has argued the profits of slavery played a crucial role in the process.

So we can see that Williams, Blackburn and Eltis provide different interpretations of the importance of slavery to capital accumulation. Williams claimed that the profits of the slave system, as he called it, provided a key stimulus to the Industrial Revolution and fertilised every branch of production in Britain. From the extract, we can conclude that Blackburn agrees that slavery made a substantial contribution to capitalism and that 'triangular trade' profits were important to domestic capital formation in Britain. But Blackburn revises the 'Williams thesis' and makes it more plausible, in part by analysing the quantitative data available but also by tracing closely how far the profits of slavery contributed to investment programmes in Britain. Eltis, on the other hand, argues that the significance of slavery to the British economy has been exaggerated. The West Indies and sugar, when viewed as part of the British economy and compared with other British industries, are less significant than historians have claimed and the slave trade formed a negligible share of British Atlantic trade. His table shows that the profits from sugar were not sufficient to fund the Industrial Revolution as others have claimed. Eltis also suggests that international comparisons with other slave systems, such as the French or Portuguese, show that there is no clear systematic connection between the British slave system and the development of industrialisation. Eltis concludes that the most important influence of the slave system was not economic but ideological.

Like all scholars trying to explain long-term development in modern world history, Williams, Blackburn and Eltis work within explanatory frameworks – or so-called paradigms – which have their own conceptual apparatus, focus on different material and generate their own research problems. It is not always easy to compare such works and here there is no direct ideological or theoretical confrontation between the historians in the extracts. You may find it difficult to decide whose thesis you agree with, but it is important that you try to understand the arguments and bear in mind that they should be accepted, modified or rejected in terms of their cogency and 'goodness of fit' with the evidence. One thing to note here is that both Blackburn and Eltis place emphasis on quantitative data in making their argument and it is important to utilise that material when weighing up the evidence.

SLAVE-GROWN GROCERIES AND POPULAR CONSUMPTION

You will have gathered that, from the 1700s, consumer demand for plantation staples was rising in Britain and in continental Europe's more prosperous cities. Clearly, more people were drinking sweetened tea, coffee and chocolate, using sugar to make their puddings and sweets, taking snuff and smoking pipe tobacco, but how quickly and how widely did these new consumption habits spread among the lower social strata? We tend to assume a linear progression from scarcity to abundance, from elite to mass consumption in the market for these consumer goods. But does the evidence bear this out? Let's consider first tobacco, which could be considered emblematic of 'consumer society'.

EXERCISE

Do the data for tobacco in Table 15.6 suggest a steady progression from tobacco's luxury consumption by a few to its commonplace consumption by the many?

Spend just a few minutes on this exercise.

Table 15.6   Annual per capita consumption of tea, sugar and tobacco in the UK (in lb, decadal averages)

	Tea	Sugar	Tobacco
1700s		See Table 15.7	2.3
1720s		See Table 15.7	2.3
1740s		See Table 15.7	1.65
1760s		See Table 15.7	1.5
1780s		See Table 15.7	1.0
1800s	1.42	19.12	1.11
1820s	1.24	17.83	0.79
1840s	1.54	19.45	0.91
1850s	2.24	30.3	1.1

(Sources: 1800s onwards – Mitchell and Deane, 1962, pp. 355–6; tobacco before 1800 – Goodman, 1993, p. 72)

SPECIMEN ANSWER

Not at all. Assuming the data are accurate, per capita tobacco consumption peaked in the first quarter of the eighteenth century and then steadily declined over the next century. In the 1820s, consumption per head was about a third of what it had been in the 1720s. It seems most unlikely a lot of people were still smoking, but each smoker was smoking a lot less. As we know, tobacco is habit forming; you usually either smoke or you don't. Unfortunately, the data do not tell us why tobacco consumption declined or whether a particular social strata was still smoking in the 1820s – it is always important to recognise the limitations of quantitative data as well as its advantages.

EXERCISE

There are conflicting data on per capita sugar consumption in eighteenth-century Britain, but general agreement on how much was consumed in the decades after 1800 (see Table 15.7). Does the evidence indicate a linear progression from elite to mass consumption? What would a dip in consumption suggest about the general level of prosperity? How did consumption relate to wholesale price movements as shown in Tables 15.8 and 15.9? (If you convert pounds per year into ounces per week, you will get a better sense of how much was consumed in everyday life. For those unfamiliar with imperial weights and pre-decimalised currency, there is a conversion table appended to this unit.)

Spend just a few minutes on this exercise.

Table 15.7   Alternative estimates of annual per capita sugar consumption in UK (in lb)

Noel Deerr		David Richardson		Mitchell and Deane	
1700–70	4–8	1710	6.5		
		1731	15.7		
		1741	13.9		
		1751	15.0		
		1761	18		
1770–1800	11–13	1771	23.2		
1800–44	18 or less			1800s	19.12
1845–49	22.6			1820s	17.83
				1840s	19.45
				1850s	30.3

(Sources: Deerr, 1949–50, p. 532; Richardson, 1987, pp. 112–13; Mitchell and Deane, 1962, pp. 355–6)

SPECIMEN ANSWER   Although sugar consumption increased greatly from the beginning of the period covered by the table to the end this is not a linear increase. There is a plateau between 1731 and 1751, a notable increase in the 1770s (although Richardson's estimates that suggest a peak in the 1770s appear to be overestimates) and a dip in the 1820s. Again, we cannot tell from the table which classes in society were consuming sugar and of which grades. It is likely that the elite would have consumed more sugar and of higher grades. Mitchell and Deane's figures show that there was a noticeable dip in average consumption in the 1820s when wholesale prices were tumbling (as shown in Table 15.9).

DISCUSSION   How do we explain the fact that consumption dipped while prices fell? Well, sugar, unlike bread, was something a household could go without in hard times, so its consumption was a fair proxy for the general level of prosperity. For sugar consumption to drop while prices fell is a sure sign that household budgets were tightly stretched. As you might have deduced, real wages declined in the 1820s. Sugar consumption did not start to rise until the sharp reduction of sugar duties in 1846 and the harmonisation of duties on colonial and foreign muscovado.

Why is it likely that Richardson's consumption data are overestimates? His figures were arrived at by dividing retained sugar imports by the total population, and without making any allowance for the quantity 'lost' by refining in Britain. In reducing raw sugar to its more refined grades, between a quarter and a half was skimmed off in impurities. Assuming that most consumption was of the less-refined grades, it seems reasonable to deflate Richardson's estimates by at least 20 per cent. If 20 lb of sugar per head were being consumed annually by the 1770s, that would have been just over 6 oz a week. This would have cost about 2d per head, with the average family of six spending a shilling a week on coarse sugar.

Table 15.8   Annual average sugar production of the British West Indies (tons) and wholesale price index (1700 = 100), based on current prices in the London market

	Annual average sugar production (ton)	Wholesale price index
1700–04	19,467	100
1705–09	17,729	78
1710–14	22,697	76
1715–19	31,691	77
1720–24	31,644	57
1725–29	42,875	56
1730–34	44,199	46
1735–39	41,170	51
1740–44	39,038	69
1745–49	39,383	84
1750–54	44,276	76
1755–59	55,247	90
1760–64	66,334	83
1765–69	70,436	85
1770–74	84,179	84
1775–79	72,998	109
1780–84	–	161
1785–89	–	–
1790–94	–	147
1795–99	–	193
1800–04	–	119
1805–09	151,897	90
1810–14	–	127
1815–19	156,037	113
1820–24	147,733	76
1825–29	136,546	71

(Source: Watts, 1987, pp. 288, 269)

Table 15.9   Annual price (shillings and pence per cwt) of muscovado sugar on the London market, 1665–1829, in five-year means

Years	Price	Years	Price	Years	Price
1665–69	50s 4d	1725–29	24s 3d	1785–89	N/a
1670–74	23s 6d	1730–34	20s 6d	1790–94	63s 4d
1675–79	21s 3d	1735–39	22s 0d	1795–99	83s 4d
1680–84	20s 3d	1740–44	29s 9d	1800–04	51s 4d
1685–89	21s 6d	1745–49	36s 6d	1805–09	39s 0d
1690–94	35s 3d	1750–54	33s 0d	1810–14	54s 9d
1695–99	39s 6d	1755–59	39s 0d	1815–19	48s 9d
1700–04	43s 3d	1760–64	36s 0d	1820–24	32s 9d
1705–09	33s 6d	1765–69	36s 9d	1825–29	30s 9d
1710–14	32s 9d	1770–74	36s 3d		
1715–19	33s 4d	1775–79	46s 9d		
1720–24	24s 6d	1780–84	69s 6d		

(Source: Watts, 1987, p. 269)

Sugar consumption, retail prices and household expenditure

The history of sugar (and indeed tobacco, though it is not discussed here) is not just a matter of quantities consumed: the use, appearance and cultural meaning of the product changed greatly over the eighteenth and early nineteenth centuries. In the 1700s, and for some time thereafter, people spoke of *sugars* because there was no standardised commodity as we know it. Apart from its use as a luxury condiment, white sugar was widely prescribed as a medicine. One physician referred to 'nearly three hundred medicines made up with sugar' in a medical treatise of 1708. Another, Dr Frederick Slare, published *A Vindication of Sugars ... Dedicated to the Ladies* in 1715 which lauded the value of sugar as a dentifrice and as a cure for ailing eyes and the ailments of suckling babes (Mintz, 1985, p. 108). It was several decades before sugar acquired its banal significance as the universal, taken-for-granted sweetener.

As we have seen, mercantilist restrictions forbad processing beyond the muscovado stage in the British Caribbean, so all colonial sugar was imported in a 'raw' state and had to be refined before it was fit for the table. Sugar refining was more akin to baking and confectionery than an industrialised process, and refiners produced different grades to suit different retail markets. Households could choose – according to taste and income – between 'single', 'double' and even 'treble' refined sugar, as well as between 'lump', 'loaf' and 'powdered' sugar. Wealthy customers usually bought sugar in the form of a 14 pound loaf, which would be attractively presented, like a bouquet. ('Sugar dynasty' depicts luxury sugar consumption very nicely.) Retail prices reflected the different degrees of refinement: in 1744 and in 1771, the least refined 'ordinary' sugar retailed for 5d a pound, but a shilling a pound was being paid for a high-quality sugar loaf (Rogers, 1963 [1866–1902]). The Victorian scholar Thorold Rogers gathered fragmentary evidence on eighteenth-century retail prices for his monumental history of prices in England. This evidence indicates that the coarse grades were cheapest – and one would assume most widely available – in the early 1770s. We can be sure that by then sugar had entered popular expectations of regularly affordable creature comforts. But what did this mean in terms of eighteenth-century household expenditure?

To us, the shilling a week the average household was spending on sugar in 1770 seems so trifling as to be meaningless; for eighteenth-century wage earners, it was a sizeable proportion of disposable income. Even a badly paid worker in Britain today can earn the price of a pound of sugar in about 15 minutes; in the eighteenth century, it would have taken most workers half a day or more. Wages varied considerably between regions in 1700, though these variations had narrowed markedly by the century's end. In 1770, a London craftsman's daily wage in the building trades was just over 3s (36.67d) and a labourer's daily wage just over 2s (24.5d). Assuming a nine-hour day, the hourly wage was about 4d an hour for a skilled man, twopence ha'penny an hour for a labourer. Wages were about 30 per cent lower in the provinces. Money wages were quite rigid during the eighteenth century, though their purchasing power improved considerably with falling prices after 1725 and deteriorated with rising prices after 1770. In the south of England, real wages were generally lower in 1800 than they had been in 1700, though in the north they had risen by 50 or 60 per cent (Deane and Cole, 1967, pp. 18–21). Many workers – including those in urban trades – received payments in kind, so their real income when in work was more than their weekly wage, but only a fortunate minority were fully employed throughout the year. Essential food, rent and clothing probably accounted for two-thirds of all consumption expenditure in eighteenth-century Britain, with bread being by far the most important item in the average household budget. Bread was expensive in relation to workers' wages: a London labourer had to work more than two and half hours to buy a 4 lb loaf in the 1780s (see Table 15.10). A family of six needed two to three such loaves a day. Between half and three-quarters of a labourer's working time was spent earning the money to keep the family in bread. When bread prices rose steeply after 1800, the occasions when money could have been spared for sugar were few and far between.

Table 15.10   The price of bread in London (in pence (d) per 4 lb loaf)

1700s	5.25	1800s	11.96
1720s	5.26	1820s	9.94
1740s	4.76	1840s	8.6
1760s	5.74	1850s	9.46
1780s	6.43		

(Source: Mitchell and Deane, 1962, pp. 497–8)

EXERCISE

From the Library website home page, select the Library Resources tab and choose Databases. Click on Eighteenth century collections online (ECCO) within the databases list. When the ECCO screen appears, search for 'author' 'Frederick Eden', the pioneer social investigator cited at the beginning of this unit who investigated the expenditure of the poor in the late 1790s. Several search results will be listed. Click on vol. 3 of *The State of the Poor* and then search for 'sugar'; you will come up with fourteen references. Go to the first on p. 710 and you will find the yearly household budget of an Epsom gardener's family. What is immediately evident about their expenditure on sugar and tea by comparison with other household expenses?

Spend about 20 minutes on this exercise.

SPECIMEN ANSWER

The family spent substantially more on tea and sugar than on rent, and more than it did on clothes, shoes or fuel. Sugar and tea, along with butter and cheese, were the third most important items of expenditure, after bread and meat. Sugar was 9d per pound – considerably more expensive than the coarse grades had been around 1770.

If you follow up 'sugar' in other household budgets in Eden's volumes, you will find that the pattern of household expenditure was generally much the same. Sweetened tea was pretty universally consumed by England's poor (though less widely drunk in Scotland and Wales) but it was also relatively expensive. Eden frequently alluded to rising prices and greater distress, and was evidently persuaded that working-class living standards were deteriorating. Whether he was right in this has been much debated by historians, but the evidence in Table 15.6 would clearly incline us to the view that daily circumstances of most consumers were becoming more straitened. Per capita consumption of sugar reached a plateau in the late 1790s, when the wholesale price of raw sugar touched a prohibitive 83s 4d per hundredweight (cwt) (as shown in Table 15.9). Sugar consumption declined in the 1820s and did not rise significantly until the 1850s. It was as if the eighteenth-century working classes had been beckoned to the emporium of consumer delights, and were then held at arm's length in the vestibule for two generations, with their modest doles of tea and sugar thinly stretched within the family until the prosperity of the 1850s. It is clear that although sugar may have been part of the labourer's diet, to him it was still a luxury item.

Whether we can sensibly speak of the *mass consumption* of sugar in Britain before the mid nineteenth century is debatable, for our judgement is bound to be affected by knowing what came later. Between 1870 and 1900, per capita consumption of sugar doubled in the UK (reaching over 90 lb per head per year at the turn of the century) principally because of the onset of mass-produced biscuits, cakes, chocolate, soft drinks and other sweetened foodstuffs. In 1900, the wholesale price of sugar was 11s 3d per cwt, which as you can see from Table 15.9 was far below eighteenth- and early nineteenth-century prices. Even when rationed during the two world wars, the passive consumption of sugar in processed food and drink meant that considerably more was consumed per head in Britain than at *any time* before 1865.

This is emphasised to put changes in eighteenth- and early nineteenth-century consumption habits within a long-term perspective. Some historians – including Blackburn – have made large claims for sugar as a supplement to the otherwise deteriorating diet of working people during early industrialisation and as a palliative for their poorer quality of life generally. These assertions seem somewhat implausible in view of the likely quantities being consumed in workers' households.

CONCLUSION

This unit has been principally concerned with economic development and socio-cultural change in Britain, which by eighteenth-century standards was an egregiously free society. Unlike a vast swathe of central and eastern Europe, it had no class of coerced producers and no caste-like groups who were poor simply because of their hereditary status. The possibility of enjoying a considerable margin over bare subsistence was open to most and much consumption was of non-essential goods that gave pleasure and/or prestige. It may seem to be stating the obvious to say that consumption was determined by the purchasing power of individuals and households, but we should not take this characteristic of modernity for granted. The medieval church had attempted to regulate consumption for theological and moral reasons. In *ancien régime* monarchies, the nobility was a closed social order with consumption rights setting it apart from the peasantry and the bourgeoisie. Britain (like the Netherlands) had become a society in which consumption largely determined status. Indeed, Britain became what has been termed a consumer society in the eighteenth century – you might like to remind yourself of this development by returning to the discussion in Unit 13. Sugar became one of the new consumer goods and was widely available – as we have seen, even the labouring poor could afford tea with sugar during much of the eighteenth century.

Viewed in a long-term and comparative perspective, eighteenth-century Britain also stands out as a society in which production and consumption had become sharply differentiated functions, and where daily activity was clearly divided between economically productive work and household consumption. This had not always been so. In the old manorial economy – which persisted over much of Europe into the early nineteenth century – the great rural majority were both producers and consumers: they produced their own subsistence, that is food, and may well have produced some essential consumer goods, such as cloth and wooden clogs, within the household. By the eighteenth century, such self-sufficiency was rarely found in Britain: nearly all production was for exchange; there was a clear division of labour between town and country, and between agriculture and urban manufacturing and services. The market for consumer goods (food and non-food) was already well organised; distribution and retailing were becoming specialised services. Shopkeepers in the larger towns and cities were as much in the vanguard of economic modernity as manufacturers: witness the many ploys adopted to attract and retain custom – glossy packaging, advertising, offering credit, selling 'loss leaders'.

For a long time, the emergence of modern consumer society in Britain was overshadowed as a subject for scholarly investigation by the Industrial Revolution, a process which brought a step change in the rate of economic growth, first in Britain, then in north-west Europe and New England. Nevertheless, a preoccupation with industrialisation has occluded the pace and scale of socio-economic change *before* technological innovation in textiles revolutionised mass manufacturing.

Much of that change was integrally related to the construction of a 'maritime-imperial system', based on naval power, merchant shipping and long-distance trade. The colonial trades were the 'rich trades', which earned large profits but required considerable capital and advanced skills in banking, insurance and the management of shipping. As our leading naval historian puts it:

> To a greater and greater extent, Britain's real wealth was generated, and seen to be generated, from a maritime system in which overseas trade created the income which paid for the Navy, merchant shipping trained the seamen which manned it, so that the Navy in turn could protect trade and the country.
>
> (Rodger, 2004, p. 108)

The most dynamic of the 'rich trades' were with the slave plantation complex, which provided British consumers with their favourite luxury goods, sugar and tobacco, and increasingly with a major industrial input – raw cotton. And we should add that the income stream from re-exporting plantation produce was vital to financing the French wars, which became a global struggle to defend and extend the 'maritime-imperial system'. So both everyday consumption in Britain, which was becoming a free-market society, and the military–fiscal power of the British imperial state, were intimately connected with slavery and slave-driven commerce.

The stark obverse of bustling consumerism and socio-economic freedom at home was black slavery in the plantation colonies. Free-market capitalism and slave-based capitalism had common ideological and institutional roots in the rights of private property. In the context of early modern Atlantic commerce, they were mutually supportive economic systems. Without slavery, the volume of Atlantic commerce would have been much smaller, and without Atlantic commerce, the extent of the market would have been much reduced. Only late in the eighteenth century, for reasons we will explore in the next unit, did the essential nexus between these systems – the Atlantic slave trade – come to seem morally intolerable, and it was another three decades before slavery was abolished in Britain's colonies.

REFERENCES

Anstey, R. (1975) *The Atlantic Slave Trade and British Abolition*, Basingstoke, Macmillan.

Berg, M. and Hudson, P. (1992) 'Rehabilitating the Industrial Revolution, *Economic History Review*, vol. 45, no. 1, pp. 24–50.

Cannadine, D. (1987) 'British history: past, present, and future?' *Past and Present*, vol. 116, pp. 131–72.

Crafts, N.F.R. (1985) *British Economic Growth During the Industrial Revolution*, Oxford, Oxford University Press.

Davis, R. (1962) 'English foreign trade, 1700–1774', *Economic History Review*, 2nd series, vol. 15, no. 2, pp. 285–303.

Deane, P. and Cole, W.A. (1967) *British Economic Growth 1688–1959*, 2nd edn, Cambridge, Cambridge University Press.

Deerr, N. (1949–50) *A History of Sugar*, 2 vols, London, Chapman and Hall.

Eden, F. (1966 [1797]) *The State of the Poor*, 3 vols, facsimile edition, London, Frank Cass.

Goodman, J. (1993) *Tobacco in History: The Cultures of Dependence*, London, Routledge.

Inikori, J.E. (2002) *Africans and the Industrial Revolution in England: A Study in International Trade and Economic Development*, Cambridge, Cambridge University Press.

Marx, K. (1976 [1867]) *Capital*, vol. 1, Harmondsworth, Penguin.

Mintz, S.W. (1985) *Sweetness and Power: The Place of Sugar in Modern History*, Viking, New York.

Mitchell, B.R. and Deane, P. (1962) *Abstract of British Historical Statistics*, Cambridge, Cambridge University Press.

O'Brien, P.K. and Engerman, S.L. (1991) 'Exports and the growth of the British economy from the Glorious Revolution to the Peace of Amiens' in Solow, B.L. (ed.) *Slavery and the Rise of the Atlantic System*, Cambridge, Cambridge University Press.

Richardson, D. (1987) 'The slave trade, sugar and British economic growth, 1748–1776' in Solow, B.L. and Engerman, S.L. (eds) *British Capitalism and Caribbean Slavery*, Cambridge, Cambridge University Press.

Rodger, N.A.M. (2004) *The Command of the Ocean: A Naval History of Britain, 1648–1815*, London, Allen Lane.

Rogers, J.E.T. (1963 [1866–1902]) *A History of Agriculture and Prices in England*, vol. 7, *1703–1793*, Vaduz, Kraus Reprint.

Rostow, W.W. (1960) *The Stages of Economic Growth: A Non-Communist Manifesto*, Cambridge, Cambridge University Press.

Schumpeter, E.B. (1960) *English Overseas Trade Statistics 1697–1808*, Oxford, Clarendon Press.

Thompson. E.P. (1968) *The Making of the English Working Class*, Harmondsworth, Penguin.

Toynbee, A. (1884) *Lectures on the Industrial Revolution in England*, London, Rivington's.

Watts, D. (1987) *The West Indies: Patterns of Development, Culture and Environmental Change Since 1492*, Cambridge, Cambridge University Press.

Williams, E. (1961 [1944]) *Capitalism and Slavery*, Chapel Hill, University of North Carolina Press reprint.

Williamson, J.G. (1987) 'Debating the British industrial revolution', *Explorations in Economic History*, 24, pp. 269–92.

APPENDIX

Britain did not adopt a decimalised currency system until 1971. Before then, £1 was equal to 20 shillings (usually written as 20/- or 20s) and there were 12 pennies (written as 12d) in every shilling. Under the imperial system of weights and measures commonly in use up to the 1970s:

16 ounces = 1 lb (453.5 grams)
14 lb = 1 stone (6.097 kilograms)
112 lb = 1 hundredweight (50.792 kilograms)
2,240 lb = 1 ton (or long ton) (1.01584 metric tons)

Bernard Waites and Amanda Goodrich

Learning outcomes

When you have finished this unit you should have the knowledge, understanding and skills needed to answer and debate the following questions and historical problems.

- Why did the Haitian slave rebellion succeed when all other slave uprisings in modern times have failed? And what was the role of the French Revolution in ensuring this success?

- How and why was the British parliament persuaded to enact the abolition of the slave trade?

- Why was there a hiatus of some two decades between abolition of the slave trade in 1807 and the launching of a mass movement in favour of slave emancipation in Britain's colonies?

- What role did slave resistance and rebellion play in persuading the British political class that colonial slavery had to be terminated?

INTRODUCTION

DVD exercise

Before embarking on this unit, you should watch 'Breaking the chains', the second slavery programme on DVD 2, which will form the basis of your work on the third section. Please make notes on these points:

- the attitude of William Wilberforce to colonial slavery after parliament abolished the slave trade in 1807

- the impact of measures to regulate and reform colonial slavery on slaves themselves

- the role of white evangelical missionaries in slave communities in the 1820s and 1830s

- the onset of a widely supported campaign to end colonial slavery in Britain after 1823 (What was its main moral source? How did it mobilise public opinion?)

- the part played by slave resistance in ending colonial slavery.

Spend about 90 minutes on this exercise.

DISCUSSION   Keep your notes to hand as you study this unit. As you will see, the unit reflects
quite closely a number of the themes raised in the programme.

From the 1780s, the Atlantic slave trade and colonial slavery in the Americas
came under sustained moral, political and revolutionary assault. This unit
focuses on three key dramas in that assault. The first was the destruction of
slavery in Europe's most valuable colony, St Domingue, which began with the
slave rebellion in August 1791 and ended with the proclamation of the
Republic of Haiti on 1 January 1804 (see Figure 16.1). The second was the
long campaign to abolish the Atlantic slave trade, which culminated in the
outlawing of the trade by the British and US legislatures in March 1807; in
Britain it was abolished by the Act for the Abolition of the Slave Trade passed
on 25 March 1807. The third was the enactment of slave emancipation in
Britain's colonial empire, which came into force in January 1834.

Is that straightforward? Let's keep things complex for a moment. It would have
been no less true to have written: 'from the 1800s, most American regions
depending on slaves to produce their export commodities entered a golden

Figure 16.1   The West Indies, *c.*1789, from James Walvin, *Atlas of Slavery*, Harlow, Pearson Education Ltd, 2006, map 48

age'. The 1807 Act did not end the slave trade, though enforcement of the Act after 1815 did make it more hazardous and costly, and, as 'Breaking the chains' made clear, emancipation did not follow automatically from abolition. With or without an external supply of slaves, slavery was an expanding system of production in the Americas during the first half of the nineteenth century. From the 1820s, the slave plantation system was extended in Spanish Cuba and Puerto Rico, the US south, and south-east Brazil. Only with hindsight can the events we shall be considering be interpreted as part of a linear and global movement 'from slavery to freedom'.

The unit is linked with all the overarching themes of A200. It examines the political, economic, religious and social beliefs and ideologies that animated the abolitionist movement, the black revolutionaries and the campaign to emancipate the slaves. It considers more briefly how abolition and emancipation impacted on the production of plantation commodities in the British Caribbean and their consumption in Britain. In terms of state formation, this unit is concerned not only with the emergence of the state of Haiti, but also with political reform in Britain and the formation of the links between civil society and political power, which, in terms of its impact on the wider world, was perhaps the more important. The emancipation of colonial slaves would not have occurred without the larger movement of political reform, which resulted in the 1832 Reform Act. Henceforth, an anti-slavery stance was integral to the remaking of Britain as an aggressively liberal state seeking a 'new world order' in which free trade and free labour could flourish; without belittling the moral force behind this stance, it is essential to observe how it served national interests.

THE ENLIGHTENMENT, EVANGELICAL CHRISTIANITY AND ANTI-SLAVERY SENTIMENT

In February 1794, the National Convention of the new French Republic voted to abolish slavery in all French territories, without compensating the slave owners. Its brief decree declared that 'all men, without distinction of colour, domiciled in the colonies, are French citizens and enjoy all the rights assured under the Constitution' (quoted in Blackburn, 1988, p. 225). The puzzling thing is not why the French revolutionaries took this step but why it took them so long to honour their libertarian principles. Europe's leading secular thinkers had long since made the intellectual case against the institution of slavery. In mid eighteenth-century France, the progressive secular thought of the radical Enlightenment was distilled in the multi-volume *Encyclopédie*, edited by Dennis Diderot and Jean le Rond d'Alembert – a stupendous collective effort to demonstrate that human affairs could and should be subject to reason and science, rather than faith and dogma. The articles on 'Esclavage' (slavery) and 'Traite des nègres' (the slave trade) were not original pieces; their author, Louis de Jaucourt, was a minor Enlightenment figure who drew heavily on Montesquieu for the first and plagiarised a contemporary Scottish jurist for the second. But publication in the *Encyclopédie* gave them a particular authority and wide currency.

EXERCISE

Turn to the extracts from these articles that are supplied as Anthology Document 4.4, 'Enlightenment definitions of slavery', and summarise their main points.

Spend about 20 minutes on this exercise.

SPECIMEN ANSWER

The main point made here is that all men were born free and equal in nature; slavery was contrary to natural and civil law. Thus the slave trade violated religion, morality, natural laws and 'all the rights of human nature'. The following points are also made in the extracts:

- The natural freedom of man is pre-Christian and requires mankind to obey only the laws of nature. But freedom in society requires obedience to the laws established by the consent of that society.

- It is a crime to strip any man of his freedom and no man can have rights of ownership over another. People should not be treated like goods and civil law does not allow them to become the property of others.

- Slavery goes against all good government.

- There is no need for slavery as everything can be achieved by free labour or machines.

- No man has the right to buy slaves or become their master. No man should be denied his freedom, which is an inalienable right. Correspondingly, the legality of slavery cannot be a matter for individual countries to decide.

- Commercial arguments that slavery is necessary to the success of the colonies are misplaced as wealth and luxury should never be acquired on the back of the infringement of the rights of mankind.

- The abolition of slavery would not ruin the colonies but would benefit them in the long run. It is freedom and industry that are the true source of wealth.

- Slaves should be set free.

Thus in the 1760s French Enlightenment thinkers were promoting ideas about slavery that would become widespread in western Europe in the following decades. Enlightened opinion in Britain was equally hostile to slavery. The Scottish political economists – pre-eminently Adam Smith (introduced to you in Unit 13) – put free labour at the moral core of their scientific enquiry into what we now call modern economic development. 'The property which every man has in his own labour,' wrote Smith in 1776, 'as it is the original foundation of all other property, so it is the most sacred and inviolable' (Smith, 1910 [1776], p. 110). Smith took this idea from John Locke, whose influence was also briefly discussed in Unit 13, but was more consistent in condemning slavery in all circumstances. Smith believed it was economically irrational, as well as immoral, to exact another person's labour by force.

EXERCISE

Turn to Anthology Document 4.5, 'Adam Smith, *An Inquiry into the Nature and Causes of the Wealth of Nations*', and consider on what grounds Smith argues against slavery.

Spend about 10 minutes on this exercise.

SPECIMEN ANSWER Smith argues against slavery on economic rather than humanitarian grounds. Here are two of the points from Smith's work:

- Slavery is less productive than free labour. Slaves have no benefit to acquire and therefore no incentive to work and can only be induced to do so by violence. Smith uses examples from Ancient Greece and Rome, very much a focus of Enlightenment thinkers.

- Men like to dominate their workers and will use slaves, over which they have greatest power, where the law allows it and the crop is suitably profitable, such as sugar.

DISCUSSION Smith was convinced that free labourers were better workers than slaves and also cheaper. This was because labourers bore the cost of their own subsistence out of their wages whereas slave owners had to bear all the costs, (food, clothing, health, etc.) of keeping slaves. Smith's arguments were used later by abolitionists to counter claims by the pro-slavery faction that abolition would reduce their profits. Indeed, the abolitionists argued, slave labour impeded the maximising of profit because it was, in the end, more expensive than free labour. By the 1820s, Smith's argument had become part of the 'common sense' of the British political class. Indeed, most economists and many legislators and public officials in Britain came to believe that slave plantation labour was inherently less productive than free labour; this was not in fact true, but it influenced the decision to end colonial slavery in the 1830s.

In the Anglophone world, intellectual arguments against slavery resonated with a widening community of anti-slavery sentiment whose principal source was evangelical Protestantism. As a religious mindset, evangelicalism is not easy to define: in the later eighteenth century, an evangelical was usually someone who had been overwhelmed by a crushing sense of personal sin and come to realise that salvation lay only in faith in the redeeming power of Christ's sacrifice. Evangelicals were energised by a moral fervour which set them apart from other Christians; they undertook good works because 'charity' – meaning selfless love of others – was Christ's injunction and because they thereby demonstrated their faith. Evangelicalism was a transatlantic phenomenon, associated both with the moral reform of the established church and the emergence of new dissenting sects (principally the Methodists, who became a separate denomination after John Wesley's death in 1791). Such sects did not agree on all doctrinal issues but most did agree that individual liberty was an inalienable and God-given right of all mankind and that all people, whatever the colour of their skin, were equal in sin and their potential for spiritual redemption. Evangelicals were much interested in converting non-Christians to Christianity and felt that slavery undermined the process of conversion.

By 1780, although commentaries were still being published on the Biblical sanctions for slavery, the balance of Protestant theology had shifted towards condemning the institution as contrary to God's will. An anti-slavery ethic had slowly evolved among the American Quakers before being transmitted back across the Atlantic. The incompatibility of slavery and slave trading with Christian principles was first urged at the yearly meeting of the Pennsylvania Society of Friends in 1688. The Quaker doctrine that all men are brothers in the

Fatherhood of God rendered slavery problematic. In 1774, the Pennsylvania and New Jersey Quakers finally resolved to exclude slave traders and slave owners from their society. Quakers formed the large majority of the committee that met in London to set up 'A Society for Effecting the Abolition of the Slave Trade' in April 1787. This was a key moment in turning anti-slavery sentiment into political action, for the society brought together dissenting tradesmen with a few upper-class evangelical Anglicans. Pre-eminent among them was Thomas Clarkson (see Figure 16.2), who gave up a glittering career in the established church to be the society's principal investigator and publicist – roles he performed with great energy and skill, becoming the indispensable pivot between anti-slavery sentiment in the country and the parliamentary elite.

Figure 16.2   Carl Frederik von Breda, *Thomas Clarkson*, 1788, oil on canvas, 90.8 x 70.5 cm. National Portrait Gallery, London. Photo: © National Portrait Gallery

Thomas Clarkson (1760–1846) was born in Wisbech and educated at the grammar school where his father, an Anglican priest, was headmaster. In 1785, he won a Cambridge University prize for an essay on the question: 'Is it lawful to enslave the unconsenting?' This was published, by a Quaker bookseller, as *An Essay on the Slavery and Commerce of the Human Species, Particularly the African*, in 1786. In the early summer of 1787, Clarkson began the exhaustive – and exhausting – investigations on behalf of the Committee for the Abolition of the Slave Trade, which took him to every slaving port. In 1789–90, he spent five months in Paris trying to persuade the National Assembly to abolish the slave trade. As well as having a crucial role in securing the 1807 Act abolishing the trade, Clarkson was instrumental in ensuring its enforcement. He attended the Paris peace conference in 1814 and the 'summit meeting' of the major states at Aix-la-Chapelle in 1818 as an unofficial ambassador for anti-slavery. With the formation of the Anti-slavery Society in 1823, Clarkson threw himself into the campaign for gradual emancipation. In the 1830s, he lent his prestige and pen to the American abolition movement, and presided over the international anti-slavery convention held in London in June 1840.

The most important 'voice' we must attend to in the struggle to deny slavery moral legitimacy is that of the slaves and former slaves themselves. Slaves had always resisted their slavery and, in inaccessible areas of the larger colonies, escaped slaves and their descendants formed 'maroon' communities. Some became more or less permanent micro-polities, grudgingly acknowledged by colonial governors. Black scholars have seen *marronage* (to use the French term) as part of a continuum of slave resistance running from petty sabotage – when slaves surreptitiously broke tools or damaged crops – to mass rebellion. This is a problematic interpretation: maroons certainly represented escape, defiance and autonomy, but they rarely questioned the legitimacy of slavery as such. Planters not infrequently used them to hunt down absconding slaves. This should not surprise us, any more than the fact that former slaves occasionally became slave owners. To comprehend slavery as an unjust and immoral institution needed a framework of understanding in which freedom was seen either as divinely willed or a universal human right. Such a framework could only come with literacy and what we call 'discursive reasoning'. By the 1780s, emancipated and educated slaves were engaging with the Bible, where they found a powerful myth of redemption from slavery in the Book of Exodus, but also with the secular rationalism of the Enlightenment. Two former slaves, Olaudah Equiano (*c*.1745–1797) and Ottobah Cugoano (born *c*.1757), who settled in England, wrote autobiographical narratives in the 1780s and both became celebrated witnesses against the slave trade at abolitionist meetings in Britain (see Figures 16.3 and 16.4).[1]

---

[1] There is conclusive documentary evidence that Equiano was born on a Carolina slave plantation and was not, as he claimed, an African of noble birth who had been kidnapped in the interior. Cugoana's account of his Fante childhood, enslavement and sale to white traders on the coast seems to be authentic.

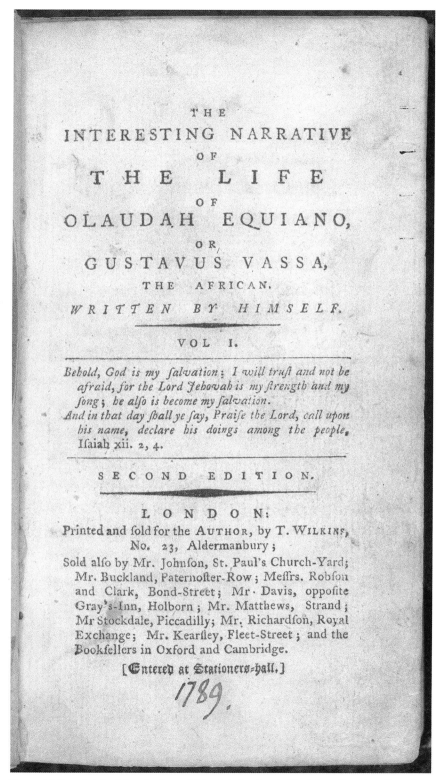

Figure 16.3a   Original frontispiece of Olaudah Equiano's *The Interesting Narrative of the Life of Olaudah Equiano, or Gustavus Vassa, The African, written by himself,* 2nd edn, London, 1787. Photo: The British Library

Figure 16.3b   Portrait of the author, Olaudah Equiano, 1789. Photo: The British Library

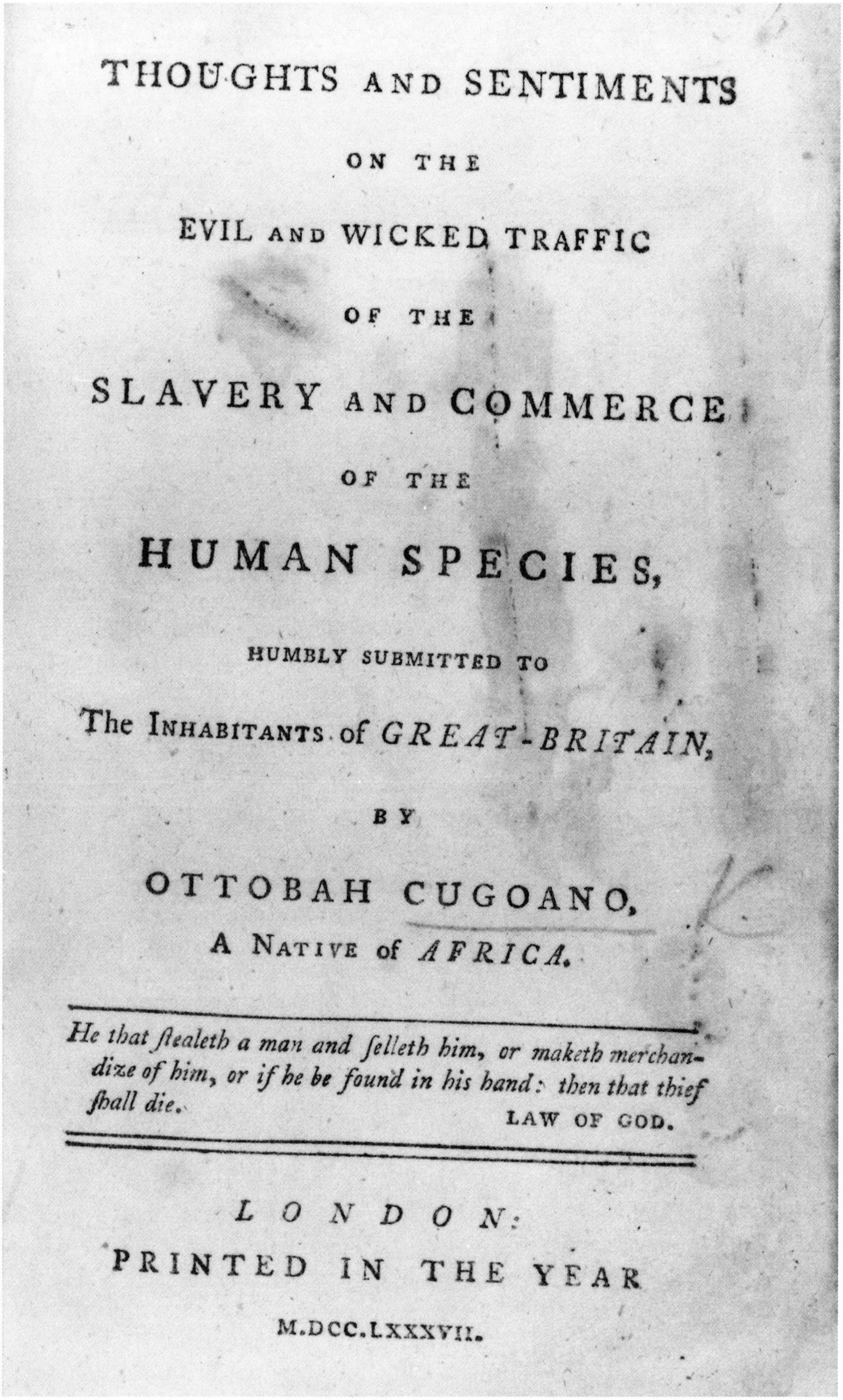

THOUGHTS AND SENTIMENTS

ON THE

EVIL AND WICKED TRAFFIC

OF THE

SLAVERY AND COMMERCE

OF THE

HUMAN SPECIES,

HUMBLY SUBMITTED TO

The INHABITANTS of GREAT-BRITAIN,

BY

OTTOBAH CUGOANO,

A NATIVE of AFRICA.

He that stealeth a man, and selleth him, or maketh merchandize of him, or if he be found in his hand: then that thief shall die.
                                                                    LAW OF GOD.

LONDON:

PRINTED IN THE YEAR

M.DCC.LXXXVII.

Figure 16.4   Ottobah Cugoano, *Thoughts and Sentiments on the Evil and Wicked Traffic of the Slavery and Commerce of the Human Species, humbly submitted to the Inhabitants of Great Britain*, London, T. Becket, etc., 1787, frontispiece. Photo: The British Library

EXERCISE

From the Library website home page, select the Library Resources tab and choose Databases. Go to Eighteenth century collections online within the databases list and find Olaudah Equiano's *The Interesting Narrative of the Life of Olaudah Equiano, or Gustavus Vassa, The African* (1789). There are a number of editions of this text on ECCO, but click on the first one and then read the address pp. (iii)–(v). Consider the following questions:

1   What is Equiano's purpose in writing this *Narrative*?

2   How does Equiano view his adopted homeland, England?

3   What sort of tone does Equiano adopt?

Spend about 20 minutes on this exercise.

SPECIMEN ANSWER

1   The aim here is to gain support for the abolition of slavery and Equiano wants to invoke compassion in his readers (and note he is addressing those in parliament) for the plight of African slaves. He is using a narrative of his life to do this and emphasises that he was torn away from his family, 'all the tender connexions' that were dear to his heart, by slave traders.

2   He claims that he has found in Britain: the Christian religion, belief in providence, and a liberal, free and enlightened society sophisticated in the arts and sciences. Here Equiano associates both Christian and Enlightenment ideas with the English nation. But clearly Equiano had his audience in mind, the educated elite, and we can surmise that this is a deliberate piece of flattery.

3   The tone is one of 'deference and respect' for the intended audience and suggests that he is inferior as an uneducated African. Such deference by those who were perceived as of lower social status was an accepted factor in eighteenth-century society. In the final paragraph it also resembles, in part, a Christian sermon with the call to God.

DISCUSSION

Equiano's *Narrative* is categorised today as a slave autobiography. Such texts generally relate the narrative of the subject's life, including their capture and sale into the slave trade, their experiences as a slave, their escape or rescue by a European and subsequent conversion to Christianity. The narratives are generally intended to create awareness of the miseries of slavery and to justify its abolition on the basis of Christian and sometimes Enlightenment beliefs and ideas. Slave autobiographies were often written with the help and guidance of a Christian benefactor and abolitionist and were promoted as propaganda for the abolitionists.

Anti-slavery sentiment had captured the moral high ground by the later eighteenth century, but had not yet made an impact on the market transactions that delivered African slaves to the Americas, and slave-grown commodities to Europe. Nor had anti-slavery sentiment effected change in the legal and political conditions that ensured these transactions were legitimate, and widely lauded as in 'the nation's interest'. It did, however, wring from a reluctant Lord Chief Justice Mansfield, in 1772, a clarification of the law respecting the right of a 'servant' to refuse forcible deportation from England. In the famous case of the absconded slave James Somerset, Mansfield ruled that there were no grounds in common law entitling Somerset's owner to force him to return to the West Indies. Mansfield did not unambiguously rule that slavery was incompatible with English law, though his judgement was generally construed in this sense. In France, there was a complete disjuncture between the anti-slavery ideology of the intellectuals and the efflorescence of colonial slavery. Slave imports into the French Antilles were never higher than in the early years of the French Revolution.

THE ST DOMINGUE REVOLUTION

On 22 August 1791, towards the close of the harvest season, an enormous slave revolt broke out in the vicinity of Le Cap (or Cap Français), the main town of St Domingue's northern plain (see Figure 16.5). Slaves armed with machetes and beating drums roamed from plantation to plantation, killing, looting and burning the cane fields. Initially, at least, they were responding to an organised conspiracy directed by elite Creole slaves. There are few undisputed facts about the prelude to the Haitian revolution, but it is generally accepted that the revolt's leaders met in the previous week to plan the uprising and take a blood oath. By the end of September, over 1,000 plantations had been destroyed, hundreds of whites killed, and tens of thousands of slaves had formed themselves into guerrilla bands. It was the largest and bloodiest slave revolt yet seen in the Americas.

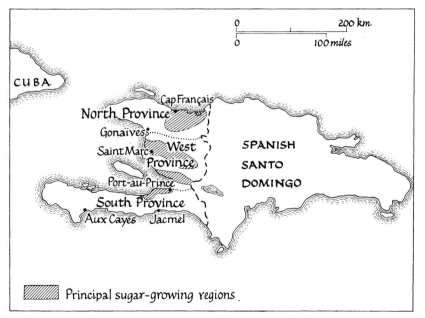

Figure 16.5   Map of St Domingue, 1790, from Philip D. Curtin, *The Rise and Fall of the Plantation Complex*, Cambridge, Cambridge University Press, 1990

What were the causes and pre-conditions for this uprising? Large-scale slave rebellions were rare events; in US history, there were many slave conspiracies but only one slave revolt involving more than 100 slaves. Some scholars have located the St Domingue rebellion in a rising tide of maroon resistance, but the evidence for this interpretation is rather slight. In the preceding decades,

St Domingue's slaves had been more quiescent than Jamaica's – although individual slaves frequently absconded, incidents of *grand marronage*, when escaped slaves formed communities that threatened planter power, were relatively few in the 1770s and 1780s. Moreover, maroon bands concentrated on the border with Spanish Santo Domingo, many miles from the revolt's epicentre on the northern plain. We may be on firmer ground in emphasising the revolt's *African* origins: huge slave imports before 1791 meant the rank-and-file insurgents were predominantly African-born young men. The revolt's organisation, and its leadership and emotional inspiration, owed much to African religious practices and beliefs. The man who gave the signal for the uprising – known to the French as Boukman – appears to have been the cult leader of a religious sect of a type ancestral to modern Haitian vodou (the preferred spelling).

However, the most important pre-condition for the revolt lay in the internecine struggle among slave owners, following the summoning of the estates general in 1788, which had undermined the structure of planter power.[2] The French colonies had not existed when this body last met and, unlike English colonies, had not developed legislative assemblies of their own. They were ruled in absolutist fashion by royal governors and officials. Summoning the estates general triggered an increasingly vicious contest over the right to political representation among the free populations of the French Antilles.[3] St Domingue's complex racial and social hierarchy, and its size and geographic diversity, made for a many-sided struggle, which no group could win single-handedly. The 30–40,000 white residents were divided on lines of social class and inherited privilege between a planter and merchant elite (the *grands blancs*, often from noble families) and an amorphous group of *petits blancs*, or poor whites, mostly estate employees, clerks, artisans and petty traders. Royal officials formed a third white group, deeply resented by Creole planters because they operated the *l'exclusif*, which denied the planters lucrative trade with foreigners, prohibited slave imports on foreign vessels (though many were smuggled in from the British Caribbean) and sacrificed their interests to those of metropolitan merchants.

Whites found some common ground in denying legal and civil equality to the roughly equal number of *gens de couleur* ('people of colour') who were nearly all of mixed race and had been formally manumitted or enjoyed de facto freedom. (The tiny numbers of free blacks were also classed as *gens de couleur*. The term 'mulatto' was often applied to the group as a whole, though strictly a mulatto was the offspring of a white and a black parent.) The economic standing of 'people of colour' in St Domingue was quite diverse: most were artisans or small traders, but they included substantial landowners who had been educated in France and were culturally indistinguishable from

---

[2] The desperate financial crisis of the French state compelled the monarchy to summon the estates general, which had not met since 1615.

[3] Limits of space preclude considering Guadeloupe and Martinique.

the white elite. About one in five slaves were owned by 'people of colour'. But whatever their wealth, the social standing of non-whites was uniformly subservient. Anyone with a trace of black ancestry was banned from public office and the professions, and forbidden to wear fine clothing, to carry weapons in town, or to sit with whites in church, at the theatre or when eating. Non-whites were, however, the main source of recruits for the militia and the *maréchaussée* (the rural police). A significant number had served in the volunteer legion sent to aid the rebellious colonists during the American War of Independence.

Whites responded to the coming of the French Revolution by clamouring for political liberty, representation and autonomy, but without conceding an iota to the free coloureds' demand for equality. In 1789, wealthy absentee planters in Paris and resident planters in St Domingue met secretly to elect deputies and ensure their representation in the French National Assembly. In early 1790, a Colonial Assembly was convened in St Marc (see Figure 16.5) which declared itself sovereign and drew up a constitution that greatly restricted metropolitan control over trade and administration. Some radical deputies – profoundly influenced by the ideological example of the American Revolution – openly discussed the idea of independence. Meanwhile, *gens de couleur* resident in France had been lobbying sympathetic deputies for a legislative proclamation that would extend citizens' rights to all freemen, whatever their colour. In March 1790, the National Assembly issued a decree on the colony's Constitution, which scrupulously ignored the question of slavery, but included a clause granting the vote to all men over 25 who fulfilled a property qualification. When it reached the Colonial Assembly in St Marc, outraged white colonists swore they would never grant political rights to a 'bastard and degenerate race' and launched a campaign of intimidation against the mulattos. In the autumn of 1790, a notable representative of the free coloureds, Vincent Ogé (*c*.1755–1791), secretly returned to St Domingue, determined to wrest equality from the whites by a show of force. He recruited a small army of free coloureds in the north and demanded the governor put an end to racial discrimination. Ogé chose his ground badly, refused to recruit any slaves, and was soon routed, but the incident spread panic among the whites and prompted savage reprisals. Ogé and a fellow conspirator were executed by being broken on the wheel.

The news of this judicial barbarity shocked the French National Assembly, where Ogé's eloquence and civility had won many admirers, and brought the colonial question to the forefront of revolutionary politics. On 15 May 1791, the National Assembly declared free coloureds born of free parents equal to whites. This was not much more than a symbolic gesture of racial solidarity, but after the declaration crossed the Atlantic it prompted a violent white backlash and incipient race war among St Domingue's free population. When the governor – bowing to white pressure – announced he would not promulgate the decree, leading mulattos in the west and south (where they outnumbered whites) formed armed bands to fight for their rights. Whites in mulatto-dominated areas were compelled to seek refuge in the larger towns. Vulnerable mulattos were massacred by white mobs. The white planter elite talked openly of secession. But whites themselves were increasingly factionalised between politically radicalised 'patriots', who sported the revolutionary tricolour, and conservative monarchists, who wore the white cockade. By August 1791, thousands of slaves had risen in rebellion.

<table>
<tr><td>

EXERCISE

</td><td>

This must be a bewildering narrative, and you probably require pause for thought. From what has been said so far, summarise the relationship between the French Revolution and the slave uprising.

</td></tr>
<tr><td>

SPECIMEN ANSWER

</td><td>

The key point is that the slaves rose as the structures of slave-owning power were dissolving into near anarchy. The solvent was the French Revolution, which had 'over-determined' events in St Domingue. It was not a direct cause of the slave uprising but it was a *necessary background condition*.

</td></tr>
</table>

Were the slave insurgents 'revolutionaries'? Objectively, perhaps, in that they were pulverising a socio-economic order, but not consciously: as far as we know, in the autumn of 1791, none were inspired by the French Revolution's ideals. In fact, the revolt's leaders tended to identify themselves as 'black royalists' because they claimed that the 'revolutionaries' in St Domingue's Colonial Assembly had suppressed a royal emancipation edict. Proclamations issued by the insurgents were usually 'in the name of the Church and King' (Geggus, 2002, p. 12). The uprising stalled when its instigator, Boukman, was captured and executed, and its leadership fell to Jean-François and Georges Biassou, who proved themselves capable military commanders, able to hold together their poorly armed and malnourished followers in remote camps. But they had no conception of a revolutionary overthrow of the colonial regime and had an ambivalent attitude to slavery as such. When, in December 1791, negotiations opened between metropolitan commissioners sent to restore order and the insurrection's leaders, the latter were willing to oversee the return of the insurgent mass to bondage provided their own freedom and that of a few hundred elite followers was guaranteed. With crass ineptitude, the white elite in the Colonial Assembly disdained this offer.

At the turn of 1791–92, few could have predicted that within two years slave emancipation would be proclaimed in the regions of the colony under the commissioners' control or that black armies led by former slaves would be major powers in the land. The insurgent slaves faced desperate problems: few knew anything of modern weaponry or military tactics; they were poorly fed and barely clothed; and the African-born were sharply divided by language and ethnicity. Once the commissioners had imposed a measure of unity on white and mulatto forces, and could dispose of French troops, the slave rebellion was fairly easily contained; thousands deserted the slave encampments and sought to return to the security of the plantations. So what determined the sequence that led to emancipation and the irruption of black military power? Part of the answer is that a core of slave insurgents remained at large in the hills and frontier zone; and we should note they found a leader of genius in Toussaint Bréda (*c.*1743–1803), better known as Toussaint Louverture ('Opening') (see Figure 16.6). But the overriding factors were the radicalisation of the French Revolution and the outbreak of international war.

Figure 16.6   Toussaint Louverture. Photo: Library of Congress

The commissioners charged with restoring metropolitan authority in St Domingue, Léger-Félicité Sonthonax and Etienne Polverel, were Jacobins[4] who imported into St Domingue a profound fear of counter-revolution. This was well founded with respect to the white elite: as the Revolution in France became virulently anti-monarchical, the *grands blancs* saw the restoration of the *ancien régime* as essential for the revival of their fortunes and social power. Some thousands of white colonists, who had been driven from their properties either by the slaves or the mulattos, took refuge in Spanish Cuba and Louisiana, and the British West Indies (see Figure 16.1 at the beginning of the unit). Like the noble émigrés who fled across France's borders in 1790, they plotted to invade St Domingue with the help of foreign aid. The news of the declaration of the Republic inspired the commissioners to destroy those institutions which might harbour royalist reaction: they dissolved the Colonial Assembly, local municipal bodies, white political clubs, and imprisoned or deported royalist officers and suspect planters. In their stead, they elevated the mulattos to the status of a new ruling class by giving them public office and command of the national guard.

The French declaration of war on the neighbouring colonial powers, Britain and Spain, in January and March 1793, accelerated in St Domingue the destruction of the white community, the transfer of power to the mulattos and the piecemeal emancipation of slaves. The endemic violence undermined slaveholding; as planters fled their properties, slaves turned themselves into squatters. Half the French soldiers sent to secure republican rule in the colony in 1792–93 died from disease within twelve months, so republican officials were compelled to recruit blacks – who were usually promised their freedom – to defend the colony against British and Spanish invaders. One stronghold of white colonists' power was eradicated when the commissioners unleashed slave prisoners and insurgents on Le Cap in June 1793. The occasion was the arrival of a new governor, who had property in St Domingue, and was believed to be sympathetic to the white counter-revolutionaries. Sonthonax attempted to arrest the new governor but was driven out by a white mob. In riposte, he issued a decree promising slave insurgents in the hinterland of Le Cap their freedom if they 'would fight for the Republic under the orders of the Civil Commissioner'. It was an invitation to sack the town, which they duly did. About 10,000 white refugees sailed for the USA. Sonthonax finally decreed general emancipation on 29 August 1793, when a British invasion was imminent. He hoped to transform the emancipated slaves into wage-serfs: tied estate workers compelled to perform paid labour. But the decree disrupted plantation discipline and encouraged black assertiveness. There is little evidence that the projected coerced labour system became a reality.

---

[4] The Jacobins were the most radical faction of the French revolutionaries; they were led by Maximilien Robespierre (1758–1794), who gained power in France in 1793.

As well as rallying the slave masses to the republican cause, the decree was intended to win over the black insurgents in the north and east, but it did not have that effect. When the Spanish invaded from Santo Domingo in May 1793, the main rebel leaders, Jean-François and Biassou, allied with Spain, as did Toussaint somewhat later. They were offered freedom, land and grand military titles in exchange for their services. The French Republic's fortunes were at a low ebb in the late summer of 1793, and there was reason to believe the colony would soon be overrun by Spain and Britain. It was not certain that the French National Convention would ratify Sonthonax's emancipation decree. Whatever might be true of their followers, the allegiance of the black commanders was not, in any event, likely to be won by this measure, since Jean-François and Biassou had sold slave women and children to the Spanish and had no principled objection to slavery. Toussaint had refused to sell slaves, which may suggest a principled objection, but the evidence is fragmentary and conflicting. He was certainly a party to the aborted agreement of December 1791, whereby the insurgent leaders would have returned their followers to bondage in exchange for securing their own freedom.

Some time in May 1794, Toussaint threw in his lot with the republicans, although for some weeks he managed to persuade the Spanish that he remained their ally. This volte-face was to be extraordinarily significant for the course of the revolution in St Domingue, because – in alliance with the republicans – Toussaint was to emerge as the colony's supreme ruler. His meteoric rise bears comparison with Napoleon's, and like Napoleon he exhibited consummate ability as a military commander, diplomat and political leader. Much is puzzling about his career, not least his reasons for switching sides in 1794. The favoured explanation is that he was persuaded to ally with the French on learning of the National Convention's decree abolishing slavery. C. L. R. James, the Afro-Caribbean Marxist, made Toussaint the flawed hero of an anti-colonial epic of social and political emancipation in *The Black Jacobins: Toussaint L'Ouverture and the San Domingo Revolution* (James, 1989 [1938]). This is a classic of black history written with great verve and insight, but archival discoveries have compelled scholars to revise several details in James's account. We now know that Toussaint had been a freeman for about twenty years at the time of the slave uprising and that he had rented and owned slaves. In law, he was an *homme de couleur*. He was a pious Catholic who spoke his father's African language more fluently than French, which he could read though barely write. Recent scholars have reinterpreted Toussaint as a man of the *ancien régime*, indifferent to modern ideology, who sought to restore the plantation economy and absolutist rule, but under a black monarch and a black plantocracy. As de facto ruler of St Domingue from 1798 to 1802, Toussaint revived the slave trade, outlawed vodou and used corporal punishment to prevent plantation workers leaving to become peasant farmers.

Very little is known about **Toussaint**'s life before the slave insurrection. He was born on the Bréda plantation in Haut-du-Cap, in the north of St Domingue, given the name Toussaint Fatras-Bâton, and raised as a household slave, not a field hand. He was manumitted in 1776 by a 'private' arrangement which avoided the fees and cumbersome procedures involved in official manumission. In 1779, he became the tenant of a small estate, owned by his son-in-law, to which thirteen slaves were attached. As a freeman and slave owner, he took no part in the early phase of the slave insurrection. The earliest document on which his name appears is an address sent by the insurgents' leaders to the Colonial Assembly in January 1792. In July 1793, after the outbreak of war with Spain, Toussaint was given a command in the forces of Spanish Santo Domingo. He went over to the French side in May 1794, and acquired the soubriquet 'Louverture' ('Opening') after breaking through the Spanish lines on several occasions. The French commissioner, Polverel, exclaimed: 'But this man's creating openings everywhere!' ('*Mais cet home fait ouverture partout!*').

Toussaint was made deputy-governor in 1796 and in the following year commander-in-chief of the French forces in the war against the British and their counter-revolutionary allies. His troops, and those of the mulatto leader André Rigaud, forced the British to evacuate the remnants of their expeditionary force (the largest yet despatched from Britain) in August 1798. Soon, the 'aristocracy' of black military officers and mulatto leaders had fallen out over who would be the new masters in St Domingue. By mid-1800, Toussaint had destroyed Rigaud's forces, compelled the leading French officials to return to France, and had brought St Domingue close to independence.

A crucial factor in his rise to undisputed power had been Britain's naval mastery of the Atlantic and Caribbean, which prevented the large-scale reinforcement of republican forces in St Domingue from France. Toussaint's fall from power resulted from the signing of the Peace of Amiens between Britain and France in 1801, and the assent given by Britain in October to a French invasion of St Domingue. Like Napoleon Bonaparte, Toussaint had appointed himself ruler for life in the summer and introduced a constitution that virtually declared St Domingue an independent state. Napoleon had married into a Creole family and had long been pressed by former planters, colonial merchants and officials to mount an expedition that would bring the upstart black to heel. What finally decided the issue was Toussaint's annexation of neighbouring Santo Domingo, where France was now the sovereign power. Led by Napoleon's brother-in-law, General Leclerc, a large French force landed in February 1802, the healthiest month for Europeans to campaign in St Domingue. The aim was to remove the black military aristocracy, restore the plantations to their former owners and institute estate serfdom. Some black commanders cooperated with Leclerc, but Toussaint and Jean-Jacques Dessalines, his principal lieutenant, retreated into the mountains, fighting a bitter rearguard action until compelled to surrender in May. Initially, Leclerc appeared willing to tolerate the black leader's presence, provided he retired to private life, but Toussaint was kidnapped and deported to France in June (with the connivance, it must be said, of Dessalines and other black generals). He died of maltreatment in a French gaol in April 1803, one of the most renowned men in the western world.

Whether Leclerc could have permanently restored French control is debatable, since yellow fever was now ravaging his forces and, fearing the return of slavery, blacks were deserting the plantations and forming guerrilla bands. On 4 July, he wrote to the minister of Marine: 'I entreat you, send me some troops. Without them I cannot undertake the disarming of the population, and without the disarming I am not master of this colony' (quoted in James, 1989 [1938], p. 336). Some days later, Leclerc was shocked to learn that the consular regime in France had restored slavery and the legality of the slave trade in the colonies with the decree of 19 May 1802. The racial discrimination of the *ancien régime* was also revived: 'people of colour' were prohibited from entering France, mixed marriages were banned and sanction given to renewed discrimination against mulattos in the French Antilles. Leclerc's instructions had not included the re-imposition of black slavery and he had repeatedly proclaimed that the Republic would respect black freedom. That commitment was essential to his pacification strategy.

| EXERCISE | Read Anthology Document 4.7, 'Letters of General Leclerc to Napoleon Bonaparte, August 1802', and summarise the impact that news of the May decree had on the French position.

Spend about 30 minutes on this exercise. |

| SPECIMEN ANSWER | Leclerc's pacification strategy was completely undermined. His 'moral force' had been destroyed; henceforth, he could rely only on brute force and that was weakening by the day because of disease in his army. The resistance of the black insurgents had become fanatical. |

Along with so many of his men, Leclerc died of yellow fever (and in despair) in early November. As his letters make clear, he relied on black and mulatto generals to hunt down insurgent bands. Before he died, the generals had turned against the French, accepted the overall leadership of Dessalines, and were providing the black insurgency with the military leadership it so desperately needed. Leclerc had resorted to indiscriminate terror; his successor, Rochambeau, openly waged a war of genocide against the black and mulatto population (Geggus, 2002, p. 26). The carnage was ended only by the resumption of war between France and Britain in May 1803, which led to the renewal of the naval blockade by the British and prevented the despatch of further French reinforcements. Napoleon had already sent 44,000 troops to St Domingue; in November, the remains of the French army were evacuated. Dessalines inaugurated the independent republic of Haiti on 1 January 1804.

Haiti was to have an ambiguous relationship with New World slavery. For blacks, it became a symbol of resistance and a haven for refugees and absconding slaves, but the destruction of Europe's richest slave colony gave a great boost to the extension of the plantation system elsewhere. The white and mixed-race planters who fled the violence took their skills and what capital they had to virgin soils: the Louisiana sugar industry was founded by St Domingan refugees; Cuba's coffee and sugar plantations were given a great fillip by the arrival of French planters and technicians, who built all the biggest sugar mills.

In Europe and North America, the Haitian revolution cast a pall over the concept of black or African self-government, not least because Dessalines ordered a massacre of all remaining whites in 1805. For much of the nineteenth century, Haiti was a pariah state: an awful warning of where slave emancipation might lead, and an embarrassment to the emancipationist cause. France refused to recognise Haiti until 1825, when it did so only after securing a massive indemnity for the destruction of French property. Until then, the French had organised an international boycott, which stifled Haitian trade. Haiti was not invited to the first congress of American states held in Panama in 1826 and not recognised by the USA until after the Civil War; the idea of black diplomats doing the rounds in Washington was unthinkable while the 'peculiar institution' of slavery flourished south of the Potomac river.

So, in this section we have considered one example of state formation in the New World. Haiti became a republic as the result of revolution among slaves and other secondary citizens, with the inadvertent assistance of European war. It could be argued that it was only the second modern state formed in the western hemisphere, and perhaps the first example of a post-colonial African state.

THE ABOLITION OF THE ATLANTIC SLAVE TRADE

Britain and the USA were not the first states to outlaw the slave trade: that accolade goes to Denmark, which prohibited Danish participation in the trade and the importation of slaves into the Danish West Indies in 1792, though the law allowed for a ten-year period of adjustment. As we have seen, the French Revolution outlawed the trade. British abolition would inevitably have greater immediate and long-term consequences for the simple reason that British slavers dominated the trade in the early 1800s. But British abolition was some time coming. One reason for this was that the pro-slavery faction fought long and hard to retain the slave trade and slavery. This faction included planters, agents and merchants in the West Indies and in Britain those who supported slavery for business, theoretical or religious reasons. They argued that abolition would damage Britain's political and economic interests. France and its Revolution posed a substantial threat to Britain during the 1790s and until the Battle of Waterloo (1815) France had denied Britain access to most European markets; anti-abolitionists argued that any move by Britain to abolish the slave trade would be advantageous to France and weaken Britain.

They also argued that Britain's global pre-eminence had been built on slavery in the West Indies. Many agreed with Edward Long (who you came across in 'Sugar dynasty') that slaves in the Caribbean were better off than the poor in England as well as Africans in Africa. Some argued that the abolition movement took the focus away from workers in Britain and their more urgent struggle against poverty and to gain political rights. Moreover, as we have seen, Long represented slaves as inferior to whites and intrinsically idle, brutish and depraved. They were only suited to slavery and were, in fact, civilised by working on the plantations. He was not alone in this idea of racial difference – David Hume had described Negroes as naturally inferior to whites in 1754 and this text was picked up by the pro-slavery faction. Christian theology was also brought to bear to support slavery. As you saw in Unit 14, the Bible was a source of justification for treating black people differently and St Augustine's writings provided a defence of slavery. Nevertheless, *why* the legislators enacted the measure *when* they did in 1807 are questions that have long intrigued historians. One answer is simply religiously inspired altruism. People certainly believed this at the time: the royal duke of Gloucester voted for the Bill in the Lords because:

> This trade is contrary to the principles of the British constitution. It is, besides, a cruel and criminal traffic in the blood of my fellow-creatures. It is a foul stain in the national character. It is an offence to the Almighty. On every ground therefore on which a decision can be made; on the ground of policy, of liberty, of humanity, of justice, but, above all, on the ground of religion, I shall vote for its immediate extinction.
>
> (Quoted in Clarkson, 1968 [1808], vol. 2, p. 571)

EXERCISE

Let us, for the moment, credit such men as the duke of Gloucester with meaning what they said; what are the problems of attributing the abolition of the slave trade simply to altruism?

Send about 15 minutes on this exercise.

SPECIMEN ANSWER

There is obviously a problem of explaining the timing. Abolitionists had occupied the moral high ground since the 1780s; their society had been active since early 1787. Why had it taken twenty years to persuade the parliamentary elite that abolition was a moral imperative? Then there is the problem of explaining how altruism came to be reconciled with the national interest.

DISCUSSION

As you have seen, the West India 'interest' had presented parliament with a wealth of evidence that abolition would subvert the plantation economy, damage British trade and play into the hands of foreign competitors. No body of legislators could lightly ignore such special pleading. As in the case of the Beckfords, slave merchants and absentee plantation owners often used their newly acquired wealth to penetrate the elite ranks of the landholding aristocracy and thus to obtain direct political influence in parliament. Indeed, by 1800 at least fifty MPs supported the pro-slavery movement.

Hindsight inevitably tempts us to see abolition as a step towards emancipation, but that is a mistaken view with respect to the British Act. As we already know from 'Breaking the chains', William Wilberforce, the Act's parliamentary sponsor, explicitly denied any intention to emancipate the slaves in the British colonies. Ending slavery – he said – had never been the purpose of the abolition movement; this was a calumny put about by its opponents. Rest assured that Wilberforce is accurately reported in the programme. In his case, the altruistic step of ending the trade has to be seen against an ideology of Christian paternalism: slaveholding was not wrong provided masters observed their duty of care and slaves observed their duty of obedience. At this stage in his life, Wilberforce did not believe in an inalienable right to freedom.

Let us revert to the problem of timing. Viewed against the length of human history, and in a broad comparative framework, it is rather striking that slave trading and slavery disappeared as quickly as they did in Euro-American societies and colonies. Anti-slavery – a principled objection to human bondage – was a modern and peculiarly western phenomenon; we find nothing comparable in other civilisations. But viewed from the perspective of Thomas Clarkson, composing his *History of the Rise, Progress, and Accomplishment of Abolition of the Atlantic Slave Trade by the British Parliament* immediately after the event, it felt like an awfully long slog.

EXERCISE

Turn to Anthology Document 4.8, 'Thomas Clarkson and the abolition movement', which contains edited extracts from Clarkson's *History*, and read from the beginning as far as paragraph 7. In these extracts, Clarkson explained why the society formed in May 1787 made abolition of the slave trade, not slave emancipation, its objective. Was it because the core members shared Wilberforce's view? (He was not a member of the committee and had not played any part in setting up the society.) What practical measures did the committee take to advance its aims? We have a modern term for bodies such as this, and the sort of politics in which they engage; what is that term? How, in general, do they work?

Spend about 1 hour on this exercise.

SPECIMEN ANSWER

Clarkson makes quite clear that the ten committee members who fixed on abolition as the society's aim were convinced that slavery itself was evil. Slaves were 'deprived of the rights of men ...'. So the committee did not identify with Wilberforce's conservative Christian paternalism; it debated whether its aim should be abolition or emancipation. It settled on abolition partly in the belief that cutting off the external supply would compel planters to improve the lot of their slaves by encouraging marriage and in other ways. Equally, it saw abolition as the more politically feasible objective: it would not interfere with the planters' property rights, and the regulation of trade with colonies was generally accepted as within the competence and the power of the metropolitan government. The committee took two practical steps: the first was to devote some of its funds to the production of *publicity material* in the form of a short pamphlet, written by Clarkson – two thousand copies were to be printed and circulated among subscribers. Second, it authorised Clarkson to *gather evidence* that could be submitted to a parliamentary committee of enquiry, which the committee members expected to result from the 'public agitation of the question'. The modern term for a body such as the society, and the way it set about achieving its end, is *pressure group politics*. Pressure groups try to *mobilise public opinion*, which is then brought to bear on legislators.

EXERCISE

You should have gathered from 'Breaking the chains' that the abolition movement perfected a particular technique in mobilising public opinion. What was it? What did it imply about the skills and social consciousness of quite ordinary people in Britain? (Read Anthology Document 4.8, 'Thomas Clarkson and the abolition movement', from paragraph 7 to the end in connection with this exercise.)

Spend about 20 minutes on this exercise.

SPECIMEN ANSWER

The mass petitioning of parliament. Abolitionist petitions were signed by hundreds of thousands of people.

As Clarkson makes clear, the society did not initiate petitioning to abolish the trade, although he was pleased to discover that others had done so. Ordinary folk in Manchester and elsewhere had taken the initiative. Why? Clarkson suggests that 'a spirit' and 'fervour' had been ignited among the people on the subject of the slave trade. Indeed due to the labours of the committee, public meetings and the publication of public prints the nature of the slave trade had 'become generally known' throughout Britain. This had spurred some to initiate petitions and this suggested that they believed collectively they could make a difference to something happening thousands of miles away and which, ostensibly, did not concern them. Petitioners demonstrated that the market had created chains of connection between themselves, as consumers, and Africans sold into slavery.

DISCUSSION

Although petitioning had long been a way of presenting the people's grievances to the monarch and parliament, and was much used by those agitating for political reform during the same period, the petitioning campaign for abolition of the slave trade reflected an important shift in the way public opinion was organised and articulated in Britain. The most intensive petitioning was in Manchester, the industrial boom town of the 1780s and 1790s, which had neither a member of parliament nor a corporate local government. Almost 11,000 men signed its petition, which probably means that two-thirds of adult males, and the bulk of working men, were signatories (Drescher, 1987, p. 201). At this point, women – along with paupers and children – were generally excluded from signing petitions and participating in local abolitionist committees. When solicited for funds, middle- and upper-class women usually contributed to a separate 'lady's subscription'. There were significant exceptions, but abolitionists around 1790 usually considered women signatories would discredit their cause. (You have seen a strong echo of this in Wilberforce's shocked reaction to the part women played in demanding immediate emancipation in the early 1820s.) Petitioning first peaked during 1791–92, when 519 abolitionist petitions, signed by about 400,000 people, were delivered to parliament from all over Britain.

The petitioners initially made little headway with the parliamentary elite. Wilberforce was known to be a sympathiser, and he wielded considerable influence through his connection with the Clapham sect of evangelical Anglicans and his close friendship with the prime minister, William Pitt.

But the gulf between Anglican parliamentarians and an abolition movement launched largely by dissenting tradesmen is evinced by the fact that Wilberforce did not join the London Abolition Committee until 1790, and kept his membership secret for a further year.

What made the political class look at the trade in a new light was the evidence – gathered by Clarkson from the muster rolls of 20,000 seamen – that disease mortality among slaving crews was draining the Royal Navy's manpower reservoir and endangering the national interest. In early 1788, after a long interview with Clarkson, Pitt asked a committee of the Privy Council to investigate the trade. The hearings did not augur well for abolition, since in the first month only witnesses interested in continuing the slave trade were summoned. Lieutenant Matthews – whose testimony you encountered in Unit 13 – was a star turn. But Clarkson restored some balance by priming hostile witnesses to appear before the committee. When the trade's apologists rushed into print a pamphlet entitled *Scriptural Researches on the Licitness of the Slave Trade*, he persuaded the Rev. James Ramsay, a prominent abolitionist, to write a rebuttal, which went to every member of parliament. In early May, Clarkson had an interview with Charles James Fox, a leading Whig MP, at which the latter endorsed total abolition.

On 9 May, the House of Commons debated the slave trade for the first time and resolved to set up its own investigative committee in the next session. Shortly after the debate, Sir William Dolben introduced a measure to limit the number of slaves that could be carried per ton on a slaving vessel and to provide bounties for captains and surgeons on slaves landed alive in the Americas. The Liverpool slave merchants petitioned angrily against Dolben's Bill and Lord Chancellor Thurlow denounced it in the House of Lords as a gross interference with legitimate trade that would hugely advantage French competitors. Pitt threatened to break up the ministry if the measure did not become law, which it duly did.

Between the summer of 1788 and April 1791, when an abolition motion was eventually debated, the abolitionists and the slave trade's supporters both sought to dominate the proceedings of the Commons committee and win over uncommitted parliamentarians. Sixty abolition witnesses were mustered and an abstract of evidence was produced astonishingly quickly in the autumn of 1790 and distributed to all MPs. Unfortunately, the abolition motion was defeated in the Commons by 163 votes to 88. As with *all* slave trade motions, the majority of MPs did not vote, let alone participate in the debate.

In order to understand the failure of the abolition motion of 1791, and the lack of engagement of MPs with the issue, it is important to consider the abolition question in a wider context. It was not the only significant issue of the day either to parliament or the public at large. In particular, as you learned in Unit 13, the French Revolution triggered a growing political reform movement in Britain and a conservative reaction. Calls for greater religious toleration were also gathering momentum. In common with the slave trade abolitionists, such movements increasingly sought the support of ordinary people and engaged them in political agitation and petitioning.

Wilberforce introduced a second abolition motion in April 1792. In his lengthy speech, he did not deny that he desired the emancipation of the slaves. 'But, alas, in their present degraded state, they were unfit for it! Liberty was the child of reason and order.' It could not flourish 'in unrestrained licentiousness'. He alluded to Denmark's 'noble example' as an encouraging sign that other nations would abandon the trade. In the ensuing debate,[5] several speakers referred to the St Domingue rebellion, but not all were apologists for the trade; in a brilliant speech, Fox asked whether any more weighty argument could be produced in favour of abolition than the horrible scenes in St Domingue. Pitt spoke long and cogently for the motion. He confessed that the civilisation of Africa 'was near his heart ... the present deplorable state of that country ... called for our generous aid, rather than justified any despair, on our part, of her recovery ...'. He concluded his speech at about six in the morning after an all-night sitting. The Commons voted by 230 to 85 in favour of an amended motion for gradual abolition. A subsequent motion proposed the immediate cessation of the trade to foreign ports and the termination of the rest of the trade by 1800; by 151 to 132, the Commons compromised on 1796.

But the Bill had to get through the Lords, who deferred it in favour of their own investigation of the slave trade. The outbreak of war against France in 1793 eroded support for abolition in the Commons and made it a less popular cause in the country. Also, at this time Pitt's government was preoccupied with trying to crush the political reform movement it saw as a major threat to stability in Britain. Wilberforce introduced an abolition motion every year between 1795 and 1799 and again in 1802; the most votes he mustered in favour was eighty-three – less than 15 per cent of MPs. His parliamentary support improved with the admission of Irish MPs to Westminster (following the 1801 Act of Union) who were generally hostile to the slave trade. For this reason, the Commons voted for an abolition motion in June 1804, but the measure fell on a technicality before being taken up by the Lords. Many of the Irish MPs then defected, after strenuous lobbying by the West India interest persuaded them that abolition represented a threat to property. In 1805, an abolition motion was again defeated.

At this point, the geo-political realities of a world at war intervened. By 1805, over half the slave trade and half the world's trade in plantation produce were in British hands; their value to British entrepreneurs had never been greater. British capitalists were extending the sugar frontier by shipping slaves to the virgin soils of Trinidad (captured in 1797) and to Dutch Guiana (captured in 1803), but it was far from certain these territories would remain British following any peace treaty. So there was a potential danger of creating future competition for the *established* Jamaican and Barbadian planters, who were enjoying high prices and easy access to European re-export markets. They

---

[5] The speeches are fully reported in Clarkson (1968 [1808]) vol. 2, pp. 355–448.

were not 'footloose' capitalists able to lay their hands on liquid assets and they preferred the security of a market monopoly to the uncertainties of moving capital and labour to new lands on the sugar frontier. They could easily be brought to see the wisdom of prohibiting the slave supply to captured foreign colonies by both British and neutral vessels. No question of interfering with legitimate commerce; it was 'in the national interest'! There was no demur when Pitt banned the trade to captured territories by Order in Council, that is to say administrative decree, and instructed the navy to interdict the neutral trade to enemy territories.

The forming of a new ministry, led by abolitionists of long standing, Fox and Lord Grenville, in February 1806, tipped the scales in favour of complete abolition. It was an uneasy coalition and prohibiting the trade was one of the few things on which contending factions agreed. However, when introducing the Foreign Slave Trade Bill to give statutory force to Pitt's administrative decree, the attorney-general made only fleeting reference to humanity. Among the Bill's supporters, there was a conspiracy of silence as to the humanitarian ideals which had, as a matter of fact, kept them plugging away at abolition for eighteen years. Wilberforce did not speak; the West India interest did not contest the measure; only forty-eight MPs bothered to vote (thirty-five for, thirteen against). The measure was more contentious in the Lords, which had many fewer members than the Commons. Sixty-one peers voted (forty-three for, eighteen against). The peers better sensed the full implications of the Bill than the Commons, but those who gave their assent mostly believed the measure, taken in the national interest, would leave the trade fundamentally intact. In fact, it brought nearly three-quarters of British slaving activities to an end (Anstey, 1975, p. 376).

Abolitionists in the ministry and on the backbenches soon secured a motion envisaging the complete closure of the trade, but could no longer plausibly claim to be acting in the 'national interest'. By any calculation, British economic interest lay in maintaining the slave trade to its own possessions while denying it to its enemies and competitors. Total abolition could only be based on the appeal to humanity and justice. Yet, the Foreign Slave Trade Act had broken a log-jam of resistance by massively curtailing hitherto legitimate commerce: since a few dozen legislators had done a good deed for base reasons, it was easier for larger numbers to honour their Christian principles. Although the West India interest and Liverpool merchants put up a stiff rearguard action, focusing their obstructive efforts on the Lords, where the 1807 Act originated, they could not seriously argue that abolition implied immediate ruin. The measure easily passed the Lords, partly because of the unanimous support of the bishops. The vote in the Commons was an overwhelming 282 for, 16 against.

EXERCISE

Re-read this section and assess the relative significance of extra-parliamentary opinion and manoeuvrings within the parliamentary elite in abolishing the slave trade.

Spend about 25 minutes on this exercise.

SPECIMEN ANSWER This is a thorny problem of historical interpretation to which there is no simple 'correct' answer. The political process at the parliamentary centre was probably more significant than the mobilisation of public opinion. The latter was immensely important in putting abolition on the political agenda, but the crucial decisions were taken by elite politicians who were culturally insulated from the great body of petitioners. Revolution and international war, rather than the state of domestic opinion, created the circumstances in which legislators first allowed an abolition measure to fail, then later to enact two which quickly ended the British trade. Of course, there was anti-slavery sentiment in parliament as well as in the country, but parliament also offered a forum for powerful vested interests, who were past masters of procrastination. Humanity and justice were, finally, the grounds on which Lords and Commons voted for complete abolition, and in this they were at one with public opinion. But the tortuous political process by which they reached this decision was located in parliament, especially in the Lords.

It is necessary, however, to add an important rider. Once abolition was accomplished, it was impossible for the government of the day to defy public opinion and soften its stance against the slave trade. In 1814, the foreign secretary, Lord Castlereagh, appeared ready to let France resume the trade in order to win other concessions from Louis XVIII at the Congress of Vienna. On short notice, the abolitionists launched a nationwide petition campaign to press for articles against the trade at the peace negotiations. In a little over a month, some 800 petitions with about 750,000 names were gathered. About one in eight adults aligned themselves with the demand for international agreements to end the slave trade (Drescher, 1986, p. 82). Though irritated by this abolitionist pressure, Castlereagh could not ignore it: he felt compelled to seek an international agreement on the slave trade as part of the peace treaty. British governments committed considerable resources – that is, taxpayers' money – to suppressing the traffic. In 1819, a separate Slave Trade Department was established in the Foreign Office to oversee the anti-slaving campaign and the African Squadron was formed to patrol the west coast of Africa. The direct costs of suppression up to 1865 were £12.4 million (Eltis, 1987, p. 93). The indirect costs, which included higher sugar prices at home, may have been around £16 million.

In the short term, abolition had few of the detrimental consequences its opponents feared. The only clear losers were the merchants – based mainly in Liverpool – directly engaged in the slave trade. The West Indian planters and their consignees (or the London merchants who handled their produce and advanced them credit) were not economically disadvantaged, though they had experienced a severe political setback. In 1815, the British West Indies produced about 54 per cent of world sugar exports – a much larger share than in 1790. Before becoming the 'workshop of the world', Britain – thanks to its slave empire – was the world's grocer: the proportion of global plantation produce being sourced by British colonies in 1815 was probably greater than the British share of world manufactured output in 1865 (Eltis, 1987, p. 6).

However, the outbreak of peace soon revealed that abolition seriously affected the capacity of the British Caribbean plantation economy to compete in international markets. Between 1807 and 1833, the combined slave population of the old and newly acquired colonies declined by 14 per cent; the fall was much sharper in what had been Dutch Guiana than in Jamaica, where numbers declined immediately after abolition because of adverse demography, and then grew very slowly. Meanwhile, the slave population of Cuba, which continued to import African slaves and was emerging as a major sugar and coffee producer, expanded rapidly. Planters' labour costs in the British Caribbean rose, relative to their competitors', and their labour supply was insufficient to keep pace with the expansion of global demand for plantation produce. While sugar output increased by about 0.5 per cent a year in the British Caribbean in the two decades after abolition, in Cuba and Brazil it increased by up to 2 per cent a year. Cheap imported slaves explain these different rates of growth. Despite the naval patrols that sought to suppress the Atlantic slave trade, it soon revived after 1815, but since more than half the slave markets in the Americas were now closed, the price of slaves on the African coast was very low. Portuguese, Brazilian and Cuban slavers were now in a buyers' market. See Table 16.1.

Table 16.1   Slave populations in Jamaica and Cuba

Jamaican slave population		Cuban slave population	
1788	226,432	1792	84,590
1800	300,000	1817	199,145
1834	310,000	1827	286,942
		1841	436,495

SLAVE EMANCIPATION IN BRITAIN'S COLONIES

DVD exercise

'Breaking the chains' offers an engaging account of emancipation, so it should not be necessary to narrate the events leading up to the Slave Emancipation Act of 1833. Using the knowledge you have gained from the programme, write brief answers to the following questions. You should also look at Anthology Document 4.9, 'Elizabeth Heyrick's call for a total end to slavery'.

1   Most of the campaigners for abolition had emancipation as their long-term goal; why was there a lull in their activities between 1807 and 1823?

2   What were the objectives of the Anti-slavery Society formed in 1823? What sort of people – in terms of their social class and ideology – would have signed up for it?

3 What challenge did the society quickly face from people it would have considered its natural supporters?

4 The programme indicates there was a striking change in slave beliefs and ideology in the twenty years before emancipation; what was it? How did it come about? What other changes in slave demography, culture and social consciousness were taking place in this period? (You will have to think for yourself about this.)

Spend about 40 minutes on this exercise, or more if you need to watch the programme again.

SPECIMEN ANSWER

1 The war and immediate postwar years were unpropitious for any popular political activity; emancipation did not become a public issue until the relaxation of government hostility to large-scale voluntary association for political ends. To which we can add that some abolitionists had naively expected slave holding to reform itself out of existence when cut off from its African supply.

2 The objectives are indicated by its full title: it was 'The Society for Mitigating and Gradually Abolishing the State of Slavery throughout the British Dominions'. Mitigation meant ameliorating the slaves' condition by the judicial regulation of corporal punishment, the prohibition of Sunday work, and widening opportunities for manumission through self-purchase. Apart from die-hards in the West India interest, just about anyone could sign up for that. The society's president was Prince William Frederick, duke of Gloucester; its vice-presidents included fourteen members of the House of Commons and five peers. The Westminster government itself was pressing the colonial assemblies to ameliorate the slaves' condition.

3 The society soon faced radical critics who demanded immediate emancipation. The most notable was the Leicester Quaker Mrs Elizabeth Heyrick,[6] who published the anonymous pamphlet *Immediate Not Gradual Emancipation* in 1824 (it was subtitled: *An Inquiry into the Shortest, Safest, and Most Effectual Means of Getting Rid of West-Indian Slavery*). Heyrick chastised the 'wise and the good' for being duped by slave holders into a gradual emancipation, which she terms a 'satanic policy'. The slave holders knew that over time the zeal would wane and impetus would fall from the movement for emancipation and that slavery might then continue through apathy. Heyrick argued for a mass boycott of slave-grown produce in the belief that, when deprived of a market for their produce, slave holders would be forced to switch to free wage labour.

4 The striking change was the Christianisation of many slaves as a result of nonconformist missionary work. Methodist missions dated back to the 1780s but became much more active with the outbreak of peace in 1815. For perfectly good reasons, the programme focuses on the Baptist mission of William Knibb, but the Methodists were the more successful denomination in terms of the numbers of converts. Probably four-fifths of slave converts were Methodists. Christianisation encouraged literacy and new forms of association, partly

---

[6] Sometimes spelt Heyricke.

because trusted slave converts were given passes that allowed them to move freely from estate to estate. Chapel congregations were communities of freedom and equality, whatever one's legal status and colour. Black slaves served as deacons – positions of honour and respect. But there were other cultural changes associated with the rapid decline in the proportion of African-born slaves: all were coming to speak the same patois. African religious practice was either disappearing or blending with Christian belief.

EXERCISE

'Breaking the chains' represents the Sam Sharpe rebellion of late December 1831, in the Montego Bay area of Jamaica, as the crucial event that compelled the Whig government under Lord Grey to move from a policy of amelioration to one of emancipation. Scepticism is the first virtue of the historian, and as budding historians you will want to know whether the programme's account of the rebellion is authentic. You can make a judgement on this from some contemporary evidence in Anthology Documents 4.10, 'Report on the Sam Sharpe rebellion, and 4.11, 'Sam Sharpe rebellion – witness testimonies and confessions from convicted prisoners, 1832'. The first piece of (very partial) testimony consists of the report of a committee of the Jamaican House of Assembly into the cause of the rebellion, which was sent to the British government in June 1832 (extracts from the report are given in Anthology Document 4.10). Appended to the brief report were the verbatim record of witnesses examined under oath and the confessions of convicted slaves, some of them under sentence of death (extracts from the witness statements are given in Anthology Document 4.11). These confessions were heard by an Anglican rector, Thomas Stewart, who was scarcely a neutral party: Anglican priests detested the nonconformist missionaries and all their work. So there must be some doubt as to whether the confessions were accurately recorded. However, internal evidence suggests they were: some are very garbled and confusing, and it is hard to believe that Stewart would have recorded them in this form had he meant to doctor the evidence. Of course, whether condemned prisoners *tell* the truth is another matter.

Now read through the report and the confessions and judge the authenticity of the programme's account for yourself. Linton's confession will be easier to follow if read last. This is a complex exercise so, rather than giving a specimen answer, we have moved straight on to a discussion.

Spend about 90 minutes on this exercise.

DISCUSSION

Given the constraints of a television narrative, the programme makers seem to have been pretty faithful to the historical record. The Colonial Assembly's report tells us as much about the temper of the beleaguered white Jamaicans as it does about the rebellion. The report considered interference by the Westminster government, coupled with the anti-slavery campaign within and outside parliament, to have been the 'most powerful cause' of the uprising. The slaves, it argued, had been deluded into believing they would be free after Christmas 1831, and had prepared to fight for this freedom if they were denied it. Nonconformist missionaries had, the report asserted, created a leadership of slave malcontents by appointing 'the artful and intelligent' to positions in the chapels. The report then refers to a fourth cause which the programme does not mention. This was 'the public discussions of the free inhabitants' regarding further measures of amelioration. 'Free people of colour' were just under 10 per cent of Jamaica's population in 1832 and considerably outnumbered whites: their demand for civil and political equality was significant in destabilising the racial hierarchy which sustained slave holding. However, the evidence does not indicate that 'free coloureds' played a significant role in the rebellion and the programme cannot be seriously faulted for ignoring them.

The interrogation and confession of Robert Gardner is probably the most detailed insider's account of the rebellion available to historians. Note that Gardner had never been flogged and claimed to have read the newspapers, which strongly suggests he was an elite domestic slave rather than a field hand. The details of his verbatim evidence vividly confirm the general accuracy of the programme's account up to the outbreak of the rising; Samuel Sharpe did bring newspapers from Montego Bay and read them to the slaves. The slaves did believe the king of England and parliament had given Jamaica freedom, which the whites were holding back. You will have noted that he called Sharpe[7] and Tharp, another slave, 'rulers'; 'rulers' here probably means lay leaders in the Baptist chapels. In his signed statement, Gardner was obviously trying to minimise his own role in the conspiracy and to shift all blame onto Sharpe's shoulders. In Gardner's account, Sharpe is not at all the saintly pacifist portrayed in the programme. You will have noticed that Gardner referred to him as 'General Sharp' – apparently without irony – and that he appeared to exercise some kind of military command over the insurgents, whom Gardner called 'General Sharp's army'. He also referred to 'a regiment of Sharp's, under the command of Captain Johnstone' rushing off to attack the Belvidere plantation and 'different regiments [being] detached to different places'. This strongly suggests that Sharpe was coordinating the uprising in military fashion, which is not at all the impression given by the programme. Have the programme makers 'sanitised' Sharpe?

Linton's confession, which was made in the presence of M'Kinley, another slave prisoner, suggests a long-standing intention to stage an uprising ('This business has been providing for for more than two or three years'). He names Gardner along with Sharpe as 'the chief heads'. According to Linton 'we were all sworn upon the Bible to do our best to drive white and free people out of this country' and the elite slaves were to become the new plantocracy, lording it over the 'common negroes, who were not to get their freedom'. Was this true? Why should a man about to be hanged make it up? Whether it was true or not, a television narrative cannot deal with this kind of complexity in the evidence. According to Linton, 'we [the slaves] heard in the newspapers, that the people in England were speaking very bold for us; we all thought the King was upon our side.' But in Linton's account it was Gardner, not Sharpe, who took the lead in conveying this message. And if his interrogator wished to know more about 'the business' he should 'go and ask Gardner and his friends that advise him'. So, apparently, Gardner was the chief conspirator. (Linton was not the only condemned slave to make this allegation: Robert Morrice, in his confession, stated: 'I never heard any one speak of rebellion in our quarter until Robert Gardner came up and put it into our heads'.)

---

[7] The spelling in Gardner's statement is Sharp; Sharpe is more usual.

To reiterate, the programme makers have generally been faithful to the historical record. But when we examine the evidence closely we can see that it has been used selectively, to offer a compelling portrait of Sharpe as a devout, non-violent martyr in a noble cause. The truth may have been more complex – and perhaps more interesting; whatever it was, it is difficult to unravel from the conflicting testimony.

Why was Samuel Sharpe's rebellion such an accelerator of history? There had been other slave disturbances in the recent past: in Demerara, in August 1823, a few thousand slave insurgents mistook 'amelioration' for emancipation and confronted the governor with a demand for their 'right'. Their protest was mercilessly crushed; about 250 slaves were killed by troops or hanged. A local court sentenced a white missionary, the Rev. John Smith, to death for complicity in the rebellion. The Privy Council commuted his sentence, but he died in gaol before the decision arrived. Smith's fate, and the burning of missionary chapels by mobs of planters, outraged British nonconformity. The events in Demerara prompted Mrs Heyrick to publish a second pamphlet in 1824, in which she contrasted the savagery of the whites with the peaceable resistance of the slaves, whom she portrayed as Christian martyrs. Yet the Demerara events did not accelerate change in the same way as Sharpe's rebellion and its ensuing repression. This was partly a matter of scale: perhaps 20–30,000 slaves were involved in the Jamaican disturbances (though we must note this was less than one in ten of the island's slaves), but more importantly its repressive aftermath reverberated with British politics in 1832 in a way that was simply not possible in 1823–24.

EXERCISE

What had changed in British politics between 1823/4 and 1831/2 to make the aftermath of Sharpe's rebellion so consequential?

Spend about 5 minutes on this exercise.

SPECIMEN ANSWER

The campaign for parliamentary reform had come to dominate British political life and to threaten the established power structure.

DISCUSSION

Edward Thompson argued that the intensity of political mobilisation brought Britain to within an ace of revolution in 1831–32 (Thompson, 1963). The Whig government under Lord Grey came into office pledged to enlarge the franchise: it finally persuaded the Tory-dominated House of Lords to pass the Reform Act in June 1832. Until then, colonial slavery was not a major preoccupation for radical reformers either within or outside parliament; indeed, militant populists – such as William Cobbett – berated the anti-slavery movement for fretting over idle blacks while condoning 'wage slavery' in Britain. However, the Anti-slavery Society – in which Methodists had become increasingly influential – had abandoned its original gradualism; in May 1830, its annual meeting voted in favour of immediate emancipation. Grey's government announced it would have nothing to do with this, though it did agree to press the colonial legislatures to enforce amelioration. The 1832 Act transformed the political terrain for the nonconformists who were now setting the pace in the Anti-slavery Society. We must recall that, before their repeal in 1828, the Test and Corporation Acts excluded nonconforming Protestants from public office and, usually, from the electoral rolls. Their righteous anger at events in Demerara in 1823 could be shrugged off by the governing oligarchy because nonconformists were not then legally part of the political nation. Nonconformist outrage at the reign of terror unleashed in Jamaica by the Anglican Colonial Church Union in early 1832, when fourteen Baptist and six Methodist chapels were destroyed, could not be so easily deflected. The 1832 Act made a significant concession to popular sovereignty by increasing the electorate and some nonconformists benefited from this change (see Unit 13). In the first elections held under the Act in December, nonconformists were key 'swing' voters in many contested urban constituencies. The Wesleyan conference had been enjoining each congregation to make petitioning for emancipation a religious obligation; in the general election, it urged Methodists to support only those parliamentary candidates who pledged themselves to end slavery immediately. Almost 200 did so. When parliament reconvened, it was inundated with emancipation petitions, signed by over one and half million people, twice the number who had voted in the elections. Even before the outcome of the election was known, the Grey government committed itself to an emancipation measure. A special cabinet committee was appointed to negotiate with the West Indian lobby (which was now seeking maximum compensation for the slave owners, rather than trying to resist the inevitable), the parliamentarians in the anti-slavery movement, and the leading Tories in the Lords. The Emancipation Bill was signed on 28 August 1833 and became operative on 1 August 1834.

Emancipation came at some cost for British taxpayers and consumers. The West Indian interest demanded £20 million compensation for the slave owners as the price for cooperating in emancipation. The government succumbed to this threat and, ignoring the protests of the more radical elements in the Anti-slavery Society, parliament voted what was an astonishingly large sum, in relation to the general level of public spending. The compensation fund represented about 45 per cent of the slaves' total market value and was distributed according to *local* prices. Slave prices were higher in Trinidad and Guiana, so there the owners received more per slave than Jamaican and Barbadian planters. Part of the indemnity came in the form of unpaid labour, which former slaves were compelled to provide the estate owners during their so-called apprenticeship. To help finance the compensation, higher sugar duties were imposed. West Indian planters retained their monopoly on the British market because duties on foreign – invariably slave-grown – sugar were kept at prohibitive levels. The dire warnings of the West India interest that plantation production was not economically viable without slavery proved entirely correct: between 1833 and the late 1840s, the British Caribbean's share of world sugar exports slumped from over one-third to about 12 per cent.

CONCLUSION

This unit has examined contrasting experiences of emancipation: St Domingue's was revolutionary, endemically violent and finally disruptive of the colonial link between Europe and the Americas; the British empire's was reformist, only sporadically violent and generally strengthened the colonial link. Because, in enacting slave emancipation, Westminster was legislating for a worldwide empire, British slave emancipation had global consequences: it provoked the Great Trek of slave-owning Dutch farmers out of Cape Colony and into what became the independent states of Transvaal and Orange Free State. British plantation islands in the Indian Ocean (principally Mauritius, acquired from France in 1815) were as much affected as those in the Caribbean. The response of colonial legislatures and British officials to the collapse of the slave labour force was to encourage the migration of African and Asian indentured workers: tens of thousands of West African contract labourers were transported to the British Caribbean in the 1840s; similar numbers left East Africa for Indian Ocean plantations. Later in the century, about two million migrant contract workers left South Asia for plantations in Trinidad, Guiana, Natal, Ceylon and Fiji to labour under conditions that were little better than slavery.

Haitian emancipation led to the formation of a weak isolated state; British emancipation was intrinsic to the reformation of Britain as a liberal state at the heart of a liberal empire. Lord Palmerston epitomised this new liberal state. He hated slavery and spent more time in his many years in government office negotiating with other governments to suppress the slave trade than on any other issue. Palmerston believed that free labour was the essential basis for a good society.

As you have learned, while actions were important in ending slavery so too were ideas – religious, political, cultural and economic. The following exercise illustrates how strong such ideas can be.

EXERCISE

In 1831, a young French lawyer, Alexis de Tocqueville, visited the USA and travelled extensively throughout the country. On his return, he published *Democracy in America*, a penetrating analysis of democratic society. The work is full of vivid observations and among the most celebrated is a comparison of Ohio and Kentucky, which have a common border along the Ohio River.

As a last exercise in this unit, read the passages from Tocqueville reprinted as Anthology Document 4.12, 'Alexis de Tocqueville, *Democracy in America*, 1835–40', and consider what he says about differing attitudes to Negroes in Ohio and Kentucky. Next, summarise his assessment of the consequences of slavery for the economy and culture of the regions he observed while travelling down the Ohio River. (To avoid confusion: Tocqueville says Kentucky was founded in 1775 and Ohio in 1787, but they were not admitted as states to the Union until 1792 and 1803, respectively.)

Spend about 30 minutes on this exercise.

SPECIMEN ANSWER

Tocqueville first compares racial prejudice in the north, where slavery is outlawed, and the south, where it continues to exist. Perhaps surprisingly he finds that Negroes are better tolerated and integrated in the south than in the north. Although Negroes in the north are ostensibly free and have the same rights in law as whites, in reality a system that we might now call apartheid exists. In the south, where slavery continues, Negroes intermix more comfortably with whites.

In Tocqueville's view, the economic consequences of slavery in Kentucky had been wholly detrimental by comparison with the free-labour regime in Ohio, which was patently more prosperous and industrially advanced. In Kentucky, slavery had discouraged white immigration and hindered agricultural 'improvement'. Moreover, the aristocratic culture of its slave-owning class appeared hostile to the acquisitive, capitalist values so evident in Ohio. From the final paragraph, one would conclude that the prospects for slave-based production around 1830 were dim: shipping, manufactures, railroads and canals were bound to concentrate in the commercially vibrant north, and attract the more enterprising individuals away from the south.

DISCUSSION

This perfectly reasonable conclusion about the economic consequences of slavery would have been entirely wrong: slave-based production in the US south was entering a golden age around 1830. It is true that industrialisation (and urbanisation) advanced more rapidly in the north, but the south was not underdeveloped by international standards in 1860. Had the Confederacy seceded peacefully, it would have been an 'advanced' industrial nation state. Among cotton textile producing states, it would have ranked sixth and among pig iron producers, eighth. Only the Union had more railroad mileage per head of population. The south in 1860 was more prosperous than France, Denmark, the German states or, indeed, any European country except England. White southerners were, on average, wealthier than their fellow citizens in the north in 1860 and white per capita income in the south was rising more rapidly.

Thus, we can see that Tocqueville's assessment of the economics of slavery was incorrect in the southern states, although that does not mean that it was incorrect in all slave societies. Moreover, Tocqueville was a political economist clearly influenced by intellectual ideas that were common in his time (recall Adam Smith's observations on the supposed economic inefficiency of slavery reproduced in Anthology Document 4.5). Here again we can see political economy influenced by the dominant Enlightenment ideology about political liberty and the natural rights of mankind. In this text Tocqueville also includes a chapter on race, in which he argues more fully that there is great prejudice against free Negroes in the northern states and deplores the existence of slavery in the modern world.

REFERENCES

Anstey, R. (1975) *The Atlantic Slave Trade and British Abolition, 1760–1810*, Basingstoke, Macmillan.

Blackburn, R. (1988) *The Overthrow of Colonial Slavery, 1776–1848*, New York, Verso.

Clarkson, T. (1968 [1808]) *The History of the Rise, Progress, and Accomplishment of Abolition of the Atlantic Slave Trade by the British Parliament*, London, Frank Cass reprint.

Curtin, P.D. (1990) *The Rise and Fall of the Plantation Complex*, Cambridge, Cambridge University Press.

Drescher, S. (1986) *Capitalism and Slavery*, Basingstoke, Macmillan.

Drescher, S. (1987) 'Paradigms tossed; capitalism and the political sources of abolition' in Solow, B. and Engerman, S.L. (eds) *British Capitalism and Caribbean Slavery: The Legacy of Eric Williams*, Cambridge, Cambridge University Press.

Eltis, D. (1987) *Economic Growth and the Ending of the Transatlantic Slave Trade*, Oxford, Oxford University Press.

Geggus, D.P. (2002) *Haitian Revolutionary Studies*, Bloomington, Indiana University Press.

James, C.L.R. (1989 [1938]) *The Black Jacobins: Toussaint L'Ouverture and the San Domingo Revolution*, London, Allison and Busby reprint.

Smith, A. (1910 [1776]) *The Wealth of Nations*, London, Everyman.

Thompson, E.P. (1963) *The Making of the English Working Class*, New York, Vintage.

Amanda Goodrich and Bernard Waites

In this block we have taken a long, hard look at Atlantic slavery: how and why it developed in the eighteenth century, its economic success, and the reasons for its demise in the nineteenth century. In this process you have studied a variety of primary and secondary sources and have combined textual analysis of documents, data and film with a broad look at slavery in the context of a modernising European world, particularly Britain. Returning to the overarching theme of modernity we considered in Unit 13, reflect for a few minutes on how slavery contributed to, and was affected by, the modernising impetus in Europe. It might help to think about this in terms of the two most prominent of the three module themes in this block: producers and consumers, and beliefs and ideologies.

The evidence provided in Units 14 and 15 shows that New World slavery made a significant contribution to Britain's economic growth in the eighteenth century. One reason that the slave trade developed when it did was the availability of credit and a modern financial system. As discussed in Unit 15, how directly slavery contributed to the Industrial Revolution is a matter of debate among historians. But, on balance, we can conclude that it did aid industrial development in Britain in some ways. New World slavery was in economic terms a modernising impulse.

EXERCISE

Think back to Unit 14 and 'Sugar dynasty': what effect did sugar production in the West Indies have on Britain?

Spend about 20 minutes on this exercise.

SPECIMEN ANSWER

Unit 14 shows that sugar, the major plantation crop of the West Indies, became a profitable commodity for investors, producers and merchants. It made some plantation owners and merchants very rich. In particular, sugar contributed to the development of the consumer society emerging in the eighteenth century. While the elite were holding polite tea parties, the evidence suggests that sweetened tea was almost ubiquitous in later eighteenth-century society and that ordinary people spent a surprisingly large proportion of their wages on sugar. The market for slave-grown groceries in Britain was symptomatic of the way the respectable habits of an emerging consumer society permeated the social strata. Also, sugar was not just imported for domestic use, Britain also had thriving export and re-export markets for unrefined and refined sugar, respectively, in particular to the Americas and Europe. Plantations, worked by slaves, were an economically viable way to produce sugar and other crops such as tobacco and cotton demanded by a consumer society.

One link you might make here is with political economists such as Adam Smith, who argued that free wage labour was more economically viable than slave labour. They were not, however, as the units stress, correct in the early nineteenth century at least. Slavery was a cheap and efficient way to produce plantation crops in the West Indies and the Americas. Nevertheless, Smith's arguments were very influential in bringing an end to slavery in British territories and it is significant that in his writings Smith linked political economy with Enlightenment humanitarian ideas about freedom. Here, ideas we link with modernity (individual liberty and the free operation of the market) influenced the demise of two long-standing economic activities – the slave trade and slavery.

Indeed, it is clear from this block that the impetus behind slavery was not purely economic but also ideological. For much of the eighteenth century, to most people in Europe, slavery was necessary to the development of colonial commerce. While concepts of freedom were well established at home, Englishmen and women did not extend these ideas to African slaves until the last decades of the eighteenth century. As you learned in Unit 14 the ideological basis for identifying slaves as 'other' was predominantly Christian. But, paradoxically, Christianity was also a major influence on the abolition and emancipation movements. It was religious belief and Enlightenment ideology that influenced ordinary people to unite and take action against slavery. As Unit 16 shows, Enlightenment ideas about natural human rights and freedoms influenced the abolition of slavery. The widespread dissemination and assertion of such ideas in Britain meant that the paradox of the coexistence of slavery and freedom in modernising European societies was finally confronted. More indirectly, the ideological debates, and in particular Enlightenment ideas, also helped shape the liberal attitudes of the British people and the liberal governments that dominated the nineteenth century (as you will see in Block 5). Enlightenment ideas were, then, very much part of a modernising world and they are still influential today.

Moreover, the material you have studied in this block, and particularly Unit 16, illustrates the importance of ideas in history and shows that they can influence and help to shape the world. In Block 5 you will learn that, while war, revolution and industrialisation all played a major part in the creation of nations, ideology was also an important factor.

The theme of state formation is less dominant in this block, but you have studied the creation of a new state, the republic of Haiti. Moreover, throughout this block we have come across ordinary people, black and white, gaining a 'voice' to bring change in politics or society.

EXERCISE	What examples of people acting collectively to achieve political aims can you identify in this block?

Spend a few minutes on this exercise.

SPECIMEN ANSWER	One example is the slave protests, particularly the St Domingue revolution and Sam Sharpe rebellion. As 'Breaking the chains' illustrated, it was again Christianity, and the increased literacy it brought with it, that helped slaves articulate grievances and join together in revolt against their condition. Two further examples can be drawn from Unit 15: the abolition and emancipation movements. Here, those who had no

power to have their views represented within the established political process influenced public opinion and parliament by uniting, publishing tracts and pamphlets and, even more emphatically, by mass petitioning.

Thus, we have glimpsed an aspect of modernity in action – the agency of ordinary people in forcing or accelerating political change. You will come across other examples of such 'people power' in Block 5.

Finally, consider this passage from the nineteenth-century liberal philosopher John Stuart Mill:

> was there ever any domination which did not appear natural to those who possessed it? There was a time when the division of mankind into two classes, a small one of masters and a numerous one of slaves, appeared, even to the most cultivated minds, to be a natural, and the only natural, condition of the human race. ... Aristotle held this opinion without doubt or misgiving; and rested it on the same premises on which the same assertion in regard to the dominion of men over women is usually based, namely that there are different natures among mankind ... But why need I go back to Aristotle? Did not the slave owners of the Southern United States maintain the same doctrine, with all the fanaticism with which men cling to the theories that justify their passions and legitimate their personal interests? Did they not call heaven and earth to witness that the dominion of the white man over the black is natural, that the black race is by nature incapable of freedom, and marked out for slavery?
>
> (Mill, 1975 [1869], p. 440)

As Mill points out, slavery had been justified since Antiquity on the grounds that there were innate natural differences between masters and slaves. In Mill's day, the subjection of women to men was justified in identical terms; he was using the speciousness of pro-slavery arguments to expose the equally dubious arguments for the political and legal subordination of women to men. This illustrates the point that ideology and mores change over time and that a shift towards modernity is not always a linear progression. As we have seen, Atlantic slavery reflected modernity in some respects but not others; it contributed to economic modernisation, while remaining ideologically backward. Similarly, in Britain women were also subjected to restricted rights and freedoms, compared with those of men, in a society increasingly focused on individual and political liberty. As we have stressed throughout the module, history is often fragmented and does not fit together neatly to reflect one clear trajectory of 'progress'.

REFERENCES

Mill, J.S. (1975 [1869]) 'The subjection of women' in *Three Essays* (with an introduction by R. Wollheim), Oxford, Oxford University Press.

FURTHER READING

Unit 13

Black, J. (1993) *The Politics of Britain, 1688–1800*, Manchester, Manchester University Press.

Curtin, P.D. (1968) 'Epidemiology and the slave trade', *Political Science Quarterly*, vol. 83, pp. 190–216.

Hampson, N. (1968) *The Enlightenment*, Harmondsworth, Penguin.

Hudson P. (1992) *The Industrial Revolution*, London, Arnold.

Turner, M.J. (1999) *British Politics in the Age of Reform*, Manchester, Manchester University Press.

Unit 14

Blackburn, R. (1997) *The Making of New World Slavery: From the Baroque to the Modern, 1492–1800*, New York, Verso.

Eltis, D. (1987) *Economic Growth and the Ending of the Atlantic Slave Trade*, Oxford, Oxford University Press.

Sheridan, R.B. (1998) 'The formation of Caribbean plantation society, 1698–1748' in Marshall, P.J. (ed.) *The Oxford History of the British Empire: The Eighteenth Century*, Oxford, Oxford University Press.

Unit 15

Blackburn, R. (1997) *The Making of New World Slavery: From the Baroque to the Modern, 1492–1800*, New York, Verso.

Eltis, D. (2000) *The Rise of African Slavery in the Americas*, Cambridge, Cambridge University Press.

McKendrick, N., Brewer, J. and Plumb, J.H. (1983) *The Birth of a Consumer Society: The Commercialization of Eighteenth-Century England*, London, Europa.

Morgan, K. (2000) *Slavery, Atlantic Trade and the British Economy, 1660–1800*, Cambridge, Cambridge University Press.

Moykr, J. (1987) 'Has the Industrial Revolution been crowded out?', *Explorations in Economic History*, vol. 24, pp. 293–319.

Unit 16

Butler, K.M. (1995) *The Economics of Emancipation: Jamaica and Barbados, 1823–1843*, Chapel Hill, University of North Carolina Press.

Davis, D.B. (1970) *The Problem of Slavery in Western Culture*, Harmondsworth, Penguin.

Davis, D.B. (1975) *The Problem of Slavery in the Age of Revolution, 1776–1823*, Ithaca, Cornell University Press.

Drescher, S. (1977) *Econocide: British Slavery in the Era of Emancipation*, Pittsburgh, University of Pittsburgh Press.

Fogel, R.W. (1989) *Without Consentor Contract: The Rise and Fall of American Slavery*, New York, Norton.

Geggus, D.P. (1982) *Slavery, War and Revolution: The British Occupation of Saint Domingue, 1793–1798*, Oxford, Clarendon Press.

Midgley, C. (1992) *Women Against Slavery: The British Campaigns, 1780–1870*, London, Routledge.

Turner, M. (1982) *Slaves and Missions: The Disintegration of Jamaican Slave Society, 1787–1834*, Chicago, University of Illinois Press.

Walvin, J. (ed.) (1982) *Slavery and British Society, 1776–1846*, Basingstoke, Macmillan.

Walvin, J. (1992) *Black Ivory: A History of British Slavery*, London, HarperCollins.

GLOSSARY

absolutism: early modern theory of government claiming that monarchs were, by divine right, entitled to rule absolutely (i.e. without reference to parliament or the assembled estates of the realm).

agency: as used in this module means power and control, independence, free from coercion or subjugation. It is used to show that black Africans did have self-determination, power and control in terms of the slave trade in Africa.

aggregate demand: the total demand for goods and services, including demand arising from export markets and investment.

Anglo-American evangelicalism: a form of evangelicalism of the later eighteenth and nineteenth centuries that differed from the earlier evangelical reform movement in certain key respects, particularly in that it represented a moral current within Anglicanism and other Protestant sects rather than within the universal Catholic Church.

autocracy: absolute rule by a single person.

bill of exchange: a written order requiring one person to make a payment to a named payee or signatory at a specified future date. It is a negotiable instrument mainly used in international trade.

chartered company/corporation: in the early modern period, a company of merchants granted exclusive commercial rights by royal charter.

chattel slavery: the ownership of one person by another; legally enforceable property rights in people. These included the right to the slaves' productive labour, the right to possess women slaves sexually, and ownership of any child born of a female slave. Slavery was therefore a perpetual status for a class of coerced workers.

commodity production: production of any goods for the market or monetary exchange.

Creole: a term defined in a number of ways but generally a person of mixed European and black descent born in the Caribbean or a descendant of European settlers in the Caribbean.

division of labour: a system in which the tasks needed to manufacture an item are performed by a number of labourers, each having a specific role and making only part of the whole item. It represents a shift from a system in which one person would perform a number of tasks to manufacture a whole item.

econometric: refers to the measurement of economic quantities; econometric history is essentially quantitative.

Gross National Product (GNP): the total market value of the goods and services produced in a designated economy in a specified time (usually a year). GNP is theoretically equivalent to gross national income; i.e. the income from the goods and services marketed in a specified time.

Gross Industrial Product (GIP): the total market value of the output of manufacturing.

l'exclusif: (French) term used for the system of mercantilist regulation in seventeenth- and eighteenth-century France.

labour productivity: the rate of output of a given unit of labour in a specified time.

manumission: legal process by which a slave was granted his or her freedom.

maroons: from the Spanish, *cimarron* (wild); applied to runaway slaves, especially those who had formed autonomous communities beyond the reach of planter power.

nonconformism: in terms of eighteenth-century religion, this refers to the faith of those who did not conform to the established Anglican Church, such as Roman Catholics, Jews and other Protestant sects. Nonconformist Protestant sects are sometimes referred to as dissenters.

primary/secondary/tertiary employment: the labour force is conventionally divided into a primary sector (agriculture, fishing, forestry), a secondary sector (manufacturing, building, mining) and a tertiary sector (services).

primitive accumulation: a Marxist term for the early stage in the development of modern capitalism when capital was accumulated by violent plunder overseas and the brutal dispossession of primary producers of their rights to common land.

slatee: term used throughout West Africa for a Muslim slave merchant.

supply and demand: supply means the goods that producers will supply at different prices; demand refers to the quantity of goods demanded by consumers at any given price. Market economics assumes that equilibrium will be achieved between supply and demand through prices.

INDEX